WHAT READERS ARE SAYING

If you are tired of hearing the same empty advice and well-meaning cheer-you-up lines when you are suffering, you need this book. Faith Doerr understands why these words feel meaningless and even make your pain worse. She takes us to God's Word, where His truth is the only place to find peace, comfort, and identity.

—**JILL LEVENHAGEN,** editor and founder, LUTHERWOMAN

Where will we turn for wisdom, comfort, or counsel within a culture of catchphrases and self-help sayings that tickle our itching ears? Too often, I've fallen for everyday platitudes (and the empty promises they contain) because of their modern-day allure of self-reliance. After all, "God won't give you more than you can handle," right? Faith Doerr courageously challenges several touchy topics like this one, uncovering commonly held myths tucked within such sayings and exposing their potential to harm, deceive, or disillusion us. She expertly maneuvers each topic of so-called self-help, skillfully debunking it through engaging stories and insightful truth, squared in Scripture and centered in Christ, our source of strength. This book will change your approach to the way you face challenges, sorrows, fears, and frustrations. The words within these pages will guide you straight into the arms of Jesus for real and lasting help and hope—in lieu of the shallow or short-lived kind you'll find in self-help sayings or cute quotes. With a personal touch, Faith will guide you to the good Word from God that's incomparably better than even the most popular platitude. She will lead you to actionable steps through summaries, practical applications, "Gentle Reminders," and "Journal Prompts." You'll likely turn to these pages time and again for powerful reminders of the truth in Christ that sets you free from toxic me-first messages amid a culture saturated with self-help. This brilliant work receives my highest recommendation!

—**DEB BURMA,** Christian author and speaker; CPH author of *Joy: A Study of Philippians*, *Be Still and Know: A Study of Rest and Refuge*, and others

WHAT READERS ARE SAYING

God's Encouraging Word provides a path to finding strength and hope in Jesus in the midst of life's challenges. Each page reflects the promise of God's unwavering love and grace paired with intentional and practical tools to bring the reader closer to Him. Whether seeking solace in times of struggle or inspiration for the journey ahead, this book will encourage readers, uplift their spirits, and renew their hearts to look to Jesus in every aspect of their lives.

—**DR. ASHTON POPPLE,** chiropractic physician

I just read a book that made me laugh, cry, and nod my head because I felt seen and understood. What's better is that I get to call the author a friend. Faith uses her life's struggles to equip her; her past pain and disillusionment make her a wise and compassionate guide. Best of all, Faith points us to Jesus and God's Word in a way that is genuine and applicable to our everyday lives. Go ahead and order several copies at once! As you read, you'll think of a dozen friends you want to gift a copy to.

—**LINDSAY HAUSCH,** Christian author and speaker; CPH author of *Take Heart: God's Comfort for Anxious Thoughts*, *God's Provision in a Wilderness World*, and others

GOD'S ENCOURAGING WORD

True Comforts When Worldly Advice Fails

FAITH DOERR

CONCORDIA PUBLISHING HOUSE • SAINT LOUIS

DEDICATION

To my husband, Preston,
for believing in this calling long before
I believed in it myself.

Published by Concordia Publishing House
3558 S. Jefferson Ave., St. Louis, MO 63118-3968
1-800-325-3040 • cph.org

Copyright © 2024 Faith Doerr

All rights reserved. No part of this publication may be reproduced, stored in a retrieval system, or transmitted, in any form or by any means, electronic, mechanical, photocopying, recording, or otherwise, without the prior written permission of Concordia Publishing House.

Scripture quotations are from the ESV® Bible (The Holy Bible, English Standard Version®), copyright © 2001 by Crossway, a publishing ministry of Good News Publishers. Used by permission. All rights reserved.

Quotation marked *TLSB* is taken from the notes from *The Lutheran Study Bible* © 2009 Concordia Publishing House. All rights reserved.

The quotation from *Luther's Works* in this publication is from *Luther's Works*, American Edition, vol. 5 © 1968 Concordia Publishing House. All rights reserved.

1 2 3 4 5 6 7 8 9 10   33 32 31 30 29 28 27 26 25 24

CONTENTS

INTRODUCTION 6

MYTH 1: Just Be Positive 10

MYTH 2: It All Starts with Me 28

MYTH 3: I Am Stronger than My Obstacles 43

MYTH 4: God Won't Give You
More than You Can Handle 56

MYTH 5: Find Your Inner Peace 74

MYTH 6: Pray Harder 88

MYTH 7: Others Have It Worse 110

MYTH 8: Be Your Own Hero 124

CONCLUSION 138

NOTES 140

ENDNOTES 142

INTRODUCTION

Hey, friend! Thank you for picking up this book. Before you start reading, though, I want to share some thoughts about this book and the reason I decided to write it.

On a beautiful fall Sunday afternoon, my dear friend and I went to a charcuterie build class. There, we were taught how to pair different meats, cheeses, nuts, and fruit while layering them beautifully to make an attractive charcuterie board. (It's adult Lunchables, and I'm forever in love.) As we sat making our boards and chatting about my upcoming manuscript deadline, a couple at the same table asked about my book. Immediately, I went into my brief explanation: "I take the most common self-help phrases, debunk the phrases, and draw attention to the toxicity of them. Then, I turn to Scripture for what we can do and say instead." One of them asked when she could buy this book because she knew she would need it. Immediately, I thought, *I need this book too!*

If you talk with someone who creates things (books, for example), they may say something like "I made it because I needed it." This rings true for me. God uses moments throughout my life to bring good. One of the good things is this book. He brought my attention to common phrases we hear almost every day and prompted me to ask the following:

Where is God here?

Where is Jesus?

The phrases discussed in this book are common, so you've either heard or said at least one of them. I confess that I've said these phrases, thinking I was offering comfort and support until someone said them to me, and I *wasn't* comforted. Every time I hear something like "God only gives us what we can handle" or "I know you feel bad, but others have it worse," I hear the nails-on-a-chalkboard sound in my head. I physically cringe. Not because they weren't trying to offer comfort, but because the people saying these things are not aware of the difference between sayings like this and genuinely helpful things to say instead.

INTRODUCTION

I couldn't get these instances out of my head. I knew I wanted to change this. And that's where the idea for this book came from.

When we are riddled with despair, sadness, grief, anxiety, inadequacy, perfectionism, or shame, we often turn to self-help media. We read books and watch Instagram feeds about how to take back our power. We watch TikToks and Instagram Reels with me-first messages. They offer quick tips and little phrases seemingly intended to make us feel worthy. These phrases, so many times, can uplift us for a moment, but they never sustain us.

These are some of the most common phrases people use to help us feel loved and overcome our moments of sadness, inadequacy, and shame. Well-intentioned as they are, such platitudes don't honor us. They give us a high that can get us through a few hours or even a few days, but in the silence of the night, when the devil comes to devour us, that mood comes crashing down.

Instead, there are words and phrases that *do* sustain, uplift, and heal: Scripture, which God has provided for us. Certain verses bring us comfort, hope, and joy, and we can call on them and God to truly hold us in moments that feel heavy and overwhelming.

From the beginning, Satan was deceptive and had Eve doubting what God said to her. We can go to chapter 3 in the book of Genesis. Satan spoke, "Did God actually say, 'You shall not eat of any tree in the garden'?" (3:1). One question plants a small seed of doubt in her mind. After Eve told him what God said, Satan proceeded to say, "You will not surely die. For God knows that when you eat of it your eyes will be opened, and you will be like God, knowing good and evil" (3:4–5). The father of lies used seemingly simple words to call God a liar.

Just like Eve, we are tempted. We fall into the trap of doubt in our sovereign Lord and wonder if we can be like God. Our flesh desires just that. Now, if I were to ask you, "Do you want to be like God?" you would probably respond with, "No. Never." Yet as this book takes us on a deeper dive into our thoughts, words, and actions, we will find that, at the heart, we do. We believe we can "fix it ourselves," we can be "independent," "rely on no one," and "control our destiny."

When Eve listened to Satan and reached for that fruit, disobeying God, sin came into this world and contaminated our very nature. Throughout the ages, sin has infiltrated many of our practices and sayings. Sayings that seem easygoing and helpful have become twisted and turned around. Instead of being comforted with truth, we are left with empty promises that are toxic to our mental health and cause unrealistic expectations of ourselves and those around us. What's worse, some of these sayings can cause us to think things about God and His Word that are false.

Instead of turning toward ourselves, we can turn to Jesus. When we see a friend struggling, wanting to help her through it can be such a wondrous thing. God created us to be in community with one another and to lean on one another. We can often become tripped up when we say things that put the light on us and our doings and not on Christ and His work for us. Biblical examples of how Jesus handled the misery and sinfulness of this world are there for us to learn. For example, He spent forty days in the wilderness, resisting temptation and not relying on His human ability but trusting the promises of God revealed in Scripture.

One of the things God reveals to us in the Bible is that *He* is our strength:

The Lord is my rock and my fortress and my deliverer; my God, my rock, in whom I take refuge, my shield, and the horn of my salvation, my stronghold. (Psalm 18:2)

My flesh and my heart may fail, but God is the strength of my heart and my portion forever. (Psalm 73:26)

Fear not, for I am with you; be not dismayed, for I am your God; I will strengthen you, I will help you, I will uphold you with My righteous right hand. (Isaiah 41:10)

Be strong and courageous. Do not fear or be in dread of them, for it is the Lord your God who goes with you. He will not leave you or forsake you. (Deuteronomy 31:6)

You now know the why for this book; here's the how. I'm a practical

INTRODUCTION

person. Give me the research and reasoning behind your idea and support it with something practical I can implement. Since that's how I'm wired, I wanted to make practicality a feature of this book. At the end of each chapter is a summary of the top points, along with things you can do and say. This is an intentional, quick reference for those times when you need a response to someone.

Use this book over and over. Feel free to read chapters out of order if a saying you struggle with is pertinent. Also, because I'm an avid journal writer, I included some journal prompts in each chapter. Use these "Gentle Reminders" within the context of the Scripture in each chapter to ponder before you reach for your favorite journal and pen. Let the prompt take you wherever your hand and heart lead you.

My prayer for this book is that it brings you to the hope we find only in Christ Jesus.

MYTH 1
JUST BE POSITIVE

"I know things are hard right now, but just remain positive."

"Think happy thoughts."

"Smile; it's not a big deal."

"You should be thankful. It could be worse!"

"Just be positive" (and its various forms) is a saying many people (myself included) use to encourage someone who's feeling down. We believe it will lift people's spirits, but it often leaves them feeling worse. I once asked a group of friends what they thought about this saying. They responded with comments of "Oh, boy. Faith, don't even start" and "This can help me how?" Then they shared personal stories with me about when they received it, why they didn't like it, and how it didn't serve them in their time of need. The floodgates had been opened.

The common phrase "Just be positive" showed up for my husband while he was working on his golf swing. As if his technique would suddenly improve if he just thought positively when he swung his driver. It left him feeling frustrated. This phrase left my friend, who was trying for a baby, feeling defeated. With tears in her eyes, she said, "You mean, if I just think positively about becoming pregnant, I'll magically see two lines on my next pregnancy test?" It left my sister, drowning in school studies, annoyed. At the time, she was working toward her bachelor's degree in biology. She rolled her eyes when I asked her for her thoughts. She wanted to know how positivity would help her remember all the chemical compounds and equations she needed for her upcoming final test. Spoiler alert: It didn't.

These people and others shared with me their vulnerable moments and how this saying left them feeling inadequate, defeated, ashamed,

MYTH 1: JUST BE POSITIVE

angry, annoyed, or frustrated that their feelings were not validated. They expressed their need for comfort, and their loved ones tried to be encouraging but resorted to using a cliché. How much easier would life be if "Just be positive" made all our worries go away? Man, how fantastic would that be? We would be able to say, "My loved one's sickness is a bad thing, but we think it's a wonderful experience!" Or "My joblessness is causing a mountain of debt, but it's all good!" We would all become like Glinda in the Wizard of Oz, waving around a wand, smiling benignly, fixing everyone's problems, or Wendy in Peter Pan, defying gravity and flying away to the land of eternal childhood.

Now, please know that I think there is a place for positive thinking and for looking for the silver lining of a dark cloud. There is a rightful place for being grateful for the blessings God has bestowed upon us and not letting despair overtake us. I mean, the opposite of positivity is negativity. Yet maybe it's not helpful to throw out a few easy words when people are struggling with something that can't be easily or quickly fixed.

WHEN IT'S ALL THAT COMES OUT

How often does the phrase "Just be positive" come out of our mouths before we even assess the situation? Before we take time to digest the gravity of the conversation, we speak as if our minds can't handle the discomfort of someone else's sadness and struggle. It's easier to tell someone to just be positive than it is to take an active listening posture to what is causing her pain and ask what we might do for her. Our knee-jerk reaction is to put a verbal Band-Aid on negative emotions. We say, "Oh, it's all good—it'll work out," instead of taking time to just listen, to just be there.

When we simply listen to people express their sadness, grief, or frustration, we allow them to process their emotions, and we honor them right where they are at that moment. Then we can, with the help of the Holy Spirit, lead them to the One who can truly comfort them in their time of need.

Not long ago, I made this misstep in a conversation with my husband, Preston. We were deciding if we should purchase a new home. While the one we live in served us well, we were outgrowing it. At the time, a house we were considering looked like it wasn't an ideal fit and would stretch our budget more than we were willing to allow. We are diligent budgeteers and fully believe in the "live below your means" motto. But about a week later, we realized that the house was potentially a gem and we may have missed out on a great find for a great price. My husband expressed regret and doubt about passing on the house. I responded, "Just be positive. It'll all work out."

Ahh, can you hear the nails on the chalkboard too? I immediately realized what I had done. I had completely ignored his feelings and implied that his concerns weren't important. I couldn't sit with my own doubt, so I responded with a flippant phrase that didn't bring him peace. In fact, it made things worse.

HAS GOD DESERTED US?

These moments lead me to the psalms where David and other psalmists express their suffering, pain, and turmoil yet always end up recognizing that they are in the arms of God. There they receive comfort, hope, and peace, even when they're in the midst of truly desperate circumstances. In Psalm 44, Israel had just suffered a national calamity, and the people did not understand why God would allow that. The psalm starts with past occasions when God had helped them:

> You with Your own hand drove out the nations, but them You planted; You afflicted the peoples, but them You set free; for not by their own sword did they win the land, nor did their own arm save them, but Your right hand and Your arm, and the light of Your face, for You delighted in them. (Psalm 44:2–3)

They didn't understand how God could do all of that and still, in this moment, allow suffering to befall them. Like the Israelites and the psalmist, we may think God has deserted us or turned against us. It's in those moments of regret, doubt, inadequacy, and turmoil that we ask, "Why, God?"

That's when we are especially vulnerable to Satan's temptations. He thrives in that climate. When we regret and doubt, we are drawing away

MYTH 1: JUST BE POSITIVE

from Christ. Often it starts small. (At least for me it does.) It goes from "I regret our decision to not buy that house" to "God won't provide for us, will He?"

Wow! We get to that spot real quick, don't we? Isn't that how Satan works, though? He takes our small doubt and plants big seeds of "Will God do it? Will He bless you with a home? He doesn't have to. Why would He bless *you*?"

Next thing you know, you're sitting on your living-room couch questioning all of God's provision for you. Do you have experiences like that? Do you ever face a difficult situation, a conflict at work, a daily trial when you've allowed one reflection to spiral into a mountain of negative thoughts?

IS IT A BAND-AID OR TRUE HEALING?

I wonder if that is why we are so quick to say "Just be positive" to our loved ones. We know firsthand the spiral of negativity that can play out and have no desire to go down that path, so we offer someone we care about the quickest Band-Aid we can think of and hope it sticks. Yet what if in those moments, when our loved one is riddled with negative emotion, we instead point them to Christ?

When my husband expressed doubt about our house decision, I wanted to help but didn't know how. I took the quick and easy route without giving it thought, responding with a cliché that can be found on home decor and gift items. I genuinely wanted to alleviate his tension and bring some form of relief and comfort. But I didn't.

I think about that conversation, and others like it, and wish I could have a redo. I wish I could have a mulligan. I wish I could have witnessed to Preston that God's provision is not a cliché on a plaque at Hobby Lobby or Target.

I might not have come to that point if the phrase "Just be positive" hadn't been a refrain during my second pregnancy. Pregnancy has a way of reminding you that your body will do whatever it needs to do to provide a healthy environment for that baby. Everyone experiences it differently. Some women look and feel like they were truly made for it. They glow and have no complications. They love the process, and the process loves them back.

My story is different, and I am not a fan of being pregnant. My feet swell so much I can't see my ankles. I am nauseated, and during those weeks, I gag at the thought, sight, or smell of chicken. All I want to do in the first trimester is sleep. And when I'm not sleeping, I contemplate throwing up now or later. I feel nauseated the other two trimesters as well. As the baby grows, I am unable to find any comfortable position to sleep in. It's not a pretty picture. But through all that discomfort, the end product is a beautiful baby handmade by God Himself. The end result outweighs the nine months leading up to holding that precious baby in my arms. Of course I'm aware of that every moment during my pregnancies—but I don't feel better when I'm told that positive thinking will make my nausea go away.

Back to that awkward morning. I was four months pregnant with our second child, Ezekiel. My belly was like a perfect little basketball—a fact that I was in no way ready to face. Like any pregnant mama, I reached for the beloved ponytail elastic band, expecting that by looping it around the button and through the buttonhole of my pants, I would get a few extra days or even a week longer out of this pair. Yet as I hooked the elastic, black ponytail band on the button of my jeans, it had a different idea. I tried again, this time placing it into the hole first and then looping it around the button. POP! It flung across the room. It took barely a second for my mind to realize what had happened. My body was telling me, "Not today, Faith." I slumped down onto my bedroom floor and started to bawl the kind of crying that is filled with exhaustion, overwhelming thoughts, and a touch of despair.

It was the third time that week that putting on an outfit had made me cry. Here I was, unable to wear my favorite jeans when I really wanted to. I always get a little boost when I put these jeans on. Do you have a pair like that? Wearing them makes you feel like nothing can wreck your day. For me, it's this pair. I wanted to fit into them so bad, but on that day, it wasn't going to happen. I knew it was coming but was in total denial it would come so soon. Yet here it was. My clothes were telling me it was time for the pregnancy jeans.

It's during times like this—when you're feeling defeated—that people like to give some kind of encouragement. "Faith, just be positive. Pregnancy doesn't last forever." "Faith, be thankful you even are pregnant. Many women don't have the honor of being a mother." Our friends and family truly want us to feel better. They want to encourage us and remind us of the blessings in our lives. Can I just say, I love that about people. How fantastic that God has given us a community to go through this life's trials and joys with.

Yet in the middle of our needs, easy responses often don't leave us feeling empowered. Instead, we feel frustrated, annoyed, or even deflated.

WHEN IT DOES MORE HARM THAN GOOD

When we say "Just be positive," we risk disregarding the feelings of the person we are trying to comfort. Anytime someone spoke these words to me while I was pregnant, I felt guilty. "I guess I can't cry right now. I should just be positive." "Being positive will get me through this moment." "Others are happy, so I should be too."

This is permission for you to stop with that feeling. Thoughts of shame, perfectionism, and doubt will never sustain you. Forcing a smile will not make the weariness or despair go away forever. If it did, we wouldn't need Christ in our lives. Why turn to the cross and the sacrifice Jesus gave for us there when we can just smile all our tears away?

Now, maybe you're not pregnant or thinking about buying a house. Instead, you are going through something else that causes people around you to tell you to just be positive. Perhaps you are in a toxic workplace with a toxic boss or coworker. Maybe it's a family situation that feels like there is no resolution in sight. Maybe it's not your job or your family; instead, you have a private matter or an illness making you struggle with your thoughts. Your mind fills with thoughts of sadness, and you tell yourself you need to be positive, to think it all away instead of dwelling on whatever emotion you are feeling. Whatever the circumstance, thinking positively will never carry us through the hard times. Sure, it may help us for a few minutes, a few hours, or even a day, but when we're on the floor bawling, it's not positive thinking that brings comfort.

It's Jesus.

GOD LEADS US TO HIS PROMISES, NOT SHAME

Paul writes this in Romans 5:3–5:

We rejoice in our sufferings, knowing that suffering produces endurance, and endurance produces character, and character produces hope, and hope does not put us to shame, because God's love has been poured into our hearts through the Holy Spirit who has been given to us.

These verses talk about rejoicing in our sufferings. Now, wait . . . I'm supposed to be *happy* about suffering? When I first read that, I laughed out loud. Really? Paul is saying when I'm going through the trials of life, I should *rejoice*? It sounds like an oxymoron, doesn't it? As we read, we learn that God works through His Word and the Holy Spirit during our suffering. It is the Word of God and the action of the Holy Spirit that produces endurance, which produces character, which produces hope. Hope in a Redeemer does not put us to *shame*.

About that word *shame*. In this world, suffering evokes shame. As a verb, the word *shame* means "to dishonor or disgrace"; as an adjective, it means "to be ashamed." Shame tells us we are unworthy of love and belonging. Satan tells us we should be disgraced and filled with dishonor and shame for who we are. While shame leads us down that negative spiral, Satan wants us to languish in our original sin. He wants us to stay in the mindset of despair and feelings of unworthiness. When we spend time feeling as if there is no hope, as if our shame condemns us, Satan jumps up and down with glee.

But in those moments of unworthiness and shame, Jesus reminds us of the work He has already done for us. He came as a baby, lived a life of obedience, then suffered, died, and rose again. He paid the price for original sin and all sin committed since. He sacrificed Himself for us, took on all the dishonor, disgrace, and shame. This defeated Satan completely and once and for all.

Through our Baptism, we are given the glorious sacrifice of our Savior—a sacrifice made for us long before we were born. With this gift, our sin is removed and replaced with the righteousness of Christ.

WE ARE UNWORTHY BUT STILL CHOSEN

When we dive into 1 Peter 2:9, we read that like the Israelites, we are the chosen people of God:

But you are a chosen race, a royal priesthood, a holy nation, a people for His own possession, that you may proclaim the excellencies of Him who called you out of darkness into His marvelous light.

We know that we were conceived and born in sin, and without Jesus, we stay stuck in that sin forever. But in the depths of our hopeless condition, Jesus reached out His hand and pulled us out of our chains. He washed away our sins and brought us into His holy family. It is in this holy family, this holy nation, that we are given the wonderful gift of community with Jesus. We are chosen by God; now we follow Christ. We belong to the true King. By faith alone, we are royalty. No matter what trial or suffering we endure on this earth, we are members of His family. Thanks be to Jesus for His incredible sacrifice so that we can rejoice and rest in that comfort.

Yet phrases like "Just be positive" can lead us down a path of unworthiness. It leads us to thoughts such as these: "I'm ashamed to dislike being pregnant." "I'm ashamed that I don't enjoy my job while others are struggling to make ends meet." "I'm ashamed that I'm frustrated with this family situation." "I'm ashamed that I can't control my depression."

Our secular world tells us through cute quotes that we can choose to not feel the emotions of sadness, despair, frustration, or annoyance. According to them, we need to be positive for the bad thing to go away, as if positivity is the magic pill that will turn our trials into triumphs or immediately shut off the tears so the world can be sunshine and rainbows. So we believe it; we push down our emotions and put on the Positive Polly attitude. Then at night, when all the busyness of the day has died down and we are alone with our thoughts, we wonder why we don't feel better.

WE ARE EVE IN THE GARDEN

Hmm . . . could it be that we are putting our worries and sorrows into the hands of a failing world? When we share that quote or think it ourselves, we are saying we have to do it all alone. I know whenever I have that thought, I am never in the frame of mind that Jesus is with me. Instead, it is the frame of mind that *I* needed to do more. I needed to power through it and get over it. I became like Eve in the Garden of Eden.

We find Eve wanting to be like God:

> But the serpent said to the woman, "You will not surely die. For God knows that when you eat of it your eyes will be opened, and you will be like God, knowing good and evil." So when the woman saw that the tree was good for food, and that it was a delight to the eyes, and that the tree was to be desired to make one wise, she took of its fruit and ate, and she also gave some to her husband who was with her, and he ate. (Genesis 3:4–6)

Eve was tempted and chose to comply. I fall into that same temptation at times. I want to take all the power and be like God. I want to control the outcome. I want to determine what will happen, when it will happen, and how.

In power-hungry moments like this, I leave no place for Jesus to comfort me or guide me. There's no place for Him to bring me peace about the situation. Instead, I push Him aside and say, "No, I just need to be positive. Then this situation will be over, and I'll be truly happy." Friend, that's not sustainable. Pushing Jesus aside doesn't bring us closer to any kind of resolution; it simply puts us farther away from our source of hope.

It bears saying here that emotions are not sinful and should not be treated as such. In our suffering, God uses emotion to strengthen our awareness of our need for Him. Paul tells us in Romans that the virtues we need are not something we acquire or develop on our own—they are gifts of the Holy Spirit. The Holy Spirit works through suffering to make us teachable so He can show us things that will help us in this life on earth. This is how God uses our suffering for good. He uses it to turn us from self-reliance to rely on Him to teach us how to endure, to develop our character, and to give us hope. More important, He uses suffering to teach us to rely on Him for healing and deliverance from the plights of mortality to the joy of our resurrection.

God holds up the mirror of His Law to show us our selfish ways. Through the Gospel of our Savior, Jesus Christ, He provides us with the means to break away from them. Once we step out of those toxic habits and mindsets—repentance, with the help of God—we can experience peace. This type of peace might not be an absence of conflict or pain; it might not be a resolution to the situation. It's the peace of Christ Jesus: His mercy and forgiveness and the knowledge that He will not let the devil and all the ugliness of this world consume us.

When God fills us with peace in Christ Jesus, the Spirit helps us develop character traits like endurance, resolve, and faith. When I think of the virtues I want my children to have, and that I want to further develop, these are always the ones that come to mind. Endurance. Character. Hope in Christ Jesus. It gives me comfort knowing that, in the midst of my trials, I'm being sharpened and shaped.

GOD USES MOMENTS OF SUFFERING TO GROUND US CLOSER TO HIM

When I think of trials and suffering that God used to instill endurance, character, and hope, I think of Jonah. Now, I know Jonah's account is familiar, but I want to give a little recap.

God sent Jonah to Nineveh to preach repentance to the people. They were a large, evil nation that was a threat to Israel. Now, when Jonah was called, he didn't jump for joy and go, "Yay! God wants to use me!" Rather, Jonah didn't want to go to Nineveh. He had absolutely no desire

GOD'S ENCOURAGING WORD

to go, and, in fact, he didn't. Jonah did his best to avoid the assignment by taking a boat ride in the opposite direction. Due to his defiance, God sent some suffering his way: a mighty storm to disturb his getaway boat. Jonah understood that the storm was from God and told the boat's crew to throw him overboard:

> **He said to them, "Pick me up and hurl me into the sea; then the sea will quiet down for you, for I know it is because of me that this great tempest has come upon you.** (Jonah 1:12)

"You don't want to go to Nineveh? All right then. I'll put you in time-out for three days." God is creative; there's no doubt about that. Jonah fervently lifted up a prayer of thanksgiving and repentance to God from inside a fish, no less. God responded by delivering Jonah back to land. Jonah then did what God had called and equipped him to do, with the help of the Holy Spirit, in Nineveh.

The Holy Spirit is working the same way in us. This life on earth is filled with trials, disappointments, and uncertainty. That is the consequence of sin—our sins, the sins others commit against us, and sometimes just living in a world ruined by sin. During this earthly life, we will never not have any of those things. Yet God uses those moments to ground us closer to Him. God gave us emotions to experience this life with. So often, I believe, we get caught up in the idea that we need to be happy at all times. It's as if we've created this rule that in order to be a *good* Christian, we can never feel doubt, sadness, or uncertainty. But we have emotions because God created us in His image. God has emotions too.

In the biblical account of Noah, we are told that the wickedness of man was great in the earth and that every intention of his heart was continually evil (see Genesis 6:5). Moses wrote, "And the Lord regretted that He had made man on the earth, and it *grieved* Him to His heart" (Genesis 6:6, emphasis added). It *grieved* Him.

Emotions are a gift from God. They are a reflection of the divine emotions that God Himself has, such as joy, anger, wrath, jealousy, and so on. They help us experience this life and communicate with others. Our loving, gracious, forgiving Lord even felt negative emotions. Can you

MYTH 1: JUST BE POSITIVE

imagine if an angel came to Him while all of this was happening and said, "Just be positive"? We laugh because we understand the silliness of that question, yet we do the same to ourselves and others around us.

JESUS WALKED THIS EARTH TOO

Because Jesus was true man, He felt all the same emotions we do. For example, when He saw Jerusalem (see Luke 19:41), He saw their coming destruction and wept for them. Jesus cared so deeply for them, as He does for us, that watching them suffer when they didn't need to brought Him to tears. He expressed His emotions. He didn't push them to the side or shed a quiet tear and then keep walking. No. He boldly felt the sadness He had for the people of Jerusalem.

Jesus also wept in the Garden of Gethsemane. He felt the weight of sin—all sin—and knew that His earthly life would end with agony, humiliation, and rejection from His own heavenly Father. The Gospel of Mark tells us that Jesus said He felt sorrow "even to death" (14:34), and Luke tells us that Jesus' emotion was so great that His sweat fell "like great drops of blood" (22:44). Matthew tells us that Jesus fell to His knees as He prayed (see Matthew 26:39). During this time, Jewish people would normally pray standing up. It was not common practice to fall to your knees, yet Jesus did. He was so filled with sorrow for what was to come that He couldn't even stand.

In His moments of anguish, Jesus prayed like we do:

In the days of His flesh, Jesus offered up prayers and supplications, with loud cries and tears, to Him who was able to save Him from death, and He was heard because of His reverence. Although He was a son, He learned obedience through what He suffered. And being made perfect, He became the source of eternal salvation to all who obey Him. (Hebrews 5:7–9)

It's hard for me to imagine Jesus crying like that. The Son of God cried loud during prayer with tears streaming down His face. He cried to God knowing that His heavenly Father could fix it and make it all go away. Yet that was not God's will for Him—or for mankind—and Jesus knew that.

But that didn't stop Jesus from crying and feeling that emotion. Friend, the Bible doesn't tell us to brush off the sadness and brush on the happy. Instead, Jesus reminds us that He knows what we are going through. He has felt the same emotion we have. He also cried out to God. He knows what it's like to want the situation to be different. For Jesus is with us, through the Lord's Supper and in His promises. Jesus tells us in John 14:16–20 that He, along with the Holy Spirit, will be with us forever, going with us through the dark times as He leads us to the light of heaven itself:

> **And I will ask the Father, and He will give you another Helper, to be with you forever, even the Spirit of truth, whom the world cannot receive, because it neither sees Him nor knows Him. You know Him, for He dwells with you and will be in you. I will not leave you as orphans; I will come to you. Yet a little while and the world will see Me no more, but you will see Me. Because I live, you also will live. In that day you will know that I am in My Father, and you in Me, and I in you.** (John 14:16–20)

I think back to times when I was on my knees in prayer with my face filled with tears. They may have been tears of exhaustion, of feeling overwhelmed, or of anxiousness. My body trembles with emotion. I feel imperfect, inadequate, and shameful. Satan likes to get me with those thoughts. He does his best work when I am in that pit of depression. In those moments, when I feel like I am failing, I have been given comfort by this passage of Jesus in the Garden of Gethsemane.

For just like Jesus in the garden before His arrest and crucifixion, we can go to God in prayer and ask Him to bring our hearts in alignment with His will. Jesus went into that garden needing strength from His Father to be able to die for us. He knew the crushing weight of sin that required His sacrifice, and only His heavenly Father could provide what He needed to go forward. After prayer, He walked out the third time and said, "Rise, let us be going; see, My betrayer is at hand" (Matthew 26:46). He wasn't dragged out of the garden, pleading with the disciples to run away with Him. Instead, He told them to get up—it's time to go. It was time to walk straight to Judas and to the cross.

MYTH 1: JUST BE POSITIVE

These accounts in the Bible prove that Jesus is relatable. In contrast, false gods are on a pedestal. They are up there, never to come down. They will never humble themselves, for they are too important to be bothered with meeting us at our level. The same is true of the platitude "Just be positive." But humbling Himself and stooping down to us is exactly what Jesus did. God the Son came to us as a human and experienced life as everyone does. He walked on the same ground, enjoyed the same celebrations, such as weddings, and experienced loss. He humbled Himself and became a man in the lowliest of circumstances. We can take comfort in knowing He knows the pain and suffering that we experience in this world.

JESUS ENGULFS US

In his first letter to the church in Corinth, Paul rebuked the Corinthians for many wrongdoings and divisions within the community. The Corinthians repented, and Paul wrote his second letter to encourage them and remind them of God's forgiveness. May we take a moment to pause and appreciate that no matter where we are in life, God will find us and show us grace. Praise be to God that we are never so far gone that Christ can't find us and bring us back to Him.

For as we share abundantly in Christ's sufferings, so through Christ we share abundantly in comfort too. (2 Corinthians 1:5)

Paul reminds his readers that Jesus suffered and died for our sins. He suffered dying on the cross and the emotional turmoil of feeling forsaken by the Father, and He carried the weight of God's wrath for so many people's sin so that through His work on the cross for us, we can have eternal life in heaven. Through His actions, we are washed clean in the sight of God. It is due to sin that we suffer on this earth. We will see it in all areas of our lives—thoughts, family, work, and even our church community. With all this sin, we can often turn to secular opinions. Ignore the sin and be positive about it. But God doesn't call us to ignore it or tell us to forget about it. He tells us to repent of it and know that Jesus took on the wrath for our sin, took our punishment, and satisfied it through His crucifixion.

As I wrote this book, I used a journaling study Bible. Study notes are not something I understood or even appreciated growing up in the faith, but now, I honestly can't imagine my life without them. When I went to look at the study notes for verse 5, I read this: "Christ's suffering engulfs our suffering, overcomes it, and is a resource of strength for all who are in distress" (*TLSB*, 1981).

Thanks be to God there are people, with the help of the Holy Spirit, out there who write so eloquently and effectively. I was immediately taken aback by the word *engulfs*. As a first-grade teacher, that's not a word I encounter very often. It got my attention, and I wanted to know more, so I googled it. Here is the definition: "sweep over and cover it completely."

I'm overwhelmed with comfort. Jesus engulfs us. He sweeps over us in our moments of disappointment, frustration, and dissatisfaction, and He fills us with His grace. Jesus takes our suffering and covers it completely. No part of our suffering is left behind. Jesus comes into our suffering, covers it with His blood, and then overcomes it completely. Nowhere in this passage does it say, "Christ's suffering gives you happy thoughts and now you can skip about your merry way." No, it gives us peace and reminds us of the ultimate source of our strength during this life's trials. Now we have the comfort that only the death and resurrection of our Lord can bring.

Friend, there will always be trials in life when thinking positive will never solve and bring restoration to. There will be times when we become angry with ourselves, our families, or situations in our lives. We will be filled with different emotions and may not handle them in healthy ways, but we have a God who loves us just the same.

There have been times in my life that I did not know how to get through. How do you think positively when a family member has passed? How do you think about positively when the world is filling up with more sin every day? How do you think about the positive when it feels like everything is going wrong? The answer: You don't. There are some situations in this life that are "only God knows why" moments. It's a sobering fact, but it's true. These times prove the gravity and seriousness of sin. Nevertheless, it may take weeks, months, or even years, but throughout our pain, God will produce in us virtues that will last this lifetime.

Friend, we don't want to be insensitive to someone's struggles. What is painful for one person may not be painful for another, but it can still be painful. This is not something we can sweep to the side and forget. Because Satan knows the weaknesses of our human nature, he entices us to stay stuck within our pain points. We become consumed with what hurts us and turn inward. Because of this, when a friend or loved one is in pain, we may not see the suffering they are going through. This disregard for their emotions brings us to the phrase "Just be positive" instead of showering them with the love that Jesus has for them.

MAY WE SHARE OUR SUFFERINGS

In 2 Corinthians 1:7, Paul reminds us that when we share in our sufferings, we can share in our comforts too. What an honor it is to have someone come and share his or her suffering with us. Please, if anyone comes to you to share in suffering, know that is not an easy thing to do. It takes a great deal of courage to be vulnerable with someone about our pain points. May we not take it lightly that another person entrusted us with that pain.

So many times, Satan wants us to hide our sufferings. "Don't tell anyone; they will never understand." "It's too silly to worry about." "Don't let people know your private business; just put on a happy face." We can become filled with these thoughts and hide ourselves from others, separating ourselves from those who might share our burdens and remind us of Christ's promises. We tidy our hair, reapply our mascara, and move throughout our day as if nothing is bothering us.

There is comfort in sharing our struggles with others. We may find that we are not alone in them. I remember the first time I told a friend that I am scared to drive in winter weather. Since I'm from Nebraska, you would think I would be a skilled driver in all types of conditions. Although I do think I'm a good driver, bad weather makes me nervous. As I told her about my nervousness, her eyes widened, and she said, "Me too! The ice is what does it for me." We then spent the next few minutes discussing different times we had felt afraid or nervous while driving.

Before speaking with her, I was filled with shame. I would tell myself, "I'm from Nebraska. I should not be nervous in snow and ice." After sharing in our pain point, I found I wasn't the only one who felt that way. I was not alone. God provides people to help us walk through it together. Through our fears and our sufferings, God helps us endure and sharpens us so that we can share our sufferings with others. In sharing our sufferings, we can share with them the joy and comfort of Jesus' sacrifice.

Sharing our sufferings also helps us remember that many are only temporary. For example, the decision about our house would be resolved, and pregnancy feels like an eternity to me, but it's only nine months. Yet some sufferings will endure throughout the rest of our earthly lives, such as the death of a loved one or a chronic illness or a chronic economic struggle. It's difficult to live with the reality that some things will never improve and may even get worse. In these situations, a friend with a similar experience can be a true blessing. Someone to cry with, to learn from, or to simply sit with can help relieve the emotional burden of loss. Your congregation or community may have support groups for those with shared loss. Consider participating. And be willing to receive care from those who want to help you.

But remember, even this earthly life is temporary—it will not last forever. What is forever is the promise Christ gives us to be with Him for eternity in heaven. He died on the cross and rose again so that we can take comfort in knowing He will come again to raise our bodies and give us new life with Him in paradise.

When acquaintances, coworkers, friends, or loved ones come forward with their pain point, may we honor them in that moment. Instead of giving them a blanket phrase that might lead them down the road of shame and fill them with thoughts of inadequacy, we can point them to the comfort that passes all human understanding. Friend, I pray that we remind them that the grace and mercy of Jesus engulfs them and share with them comfort from God's Word that truly addresses their struggle.

MYTH 1: JUST BE POSITIVE

This is a comfort that is not momentary and does not lighten the tension just a touch but will sustain them long after the conversation ends. May we give them a resource they can use again and again in every trial of their lives. May we lead them toward honoring their feelings and lifting them, with the help of the Holy Spirit, out of the pit they find themselves in and into the arms of Jesus.

PRAYER:

Heavenly Father,
I thank You for giving a purpose to our sufferings. While this world will be plagued with sin until Your Son's return, I rejoice in knowing that You will use all things for good for those who love You. Thank You for the gift of the Holy Spirit and instilling in me the virtues of faith, endurance, character, and hope in Jesus. Lastly, Lord, I thank You for the community of believers. I thank You that You gave us people we can lean on and share in our sufferings with. I pray that, as we encounter others in the midst of their pain, we bring them to You. I pray we don't diminish their emotions or their pain points but instead share with them the comfort that only Your Son's death, resurrection, and eternal life can provide.
In Jesus' name. Amen.

GENTLE REMINDERS:

- Pray with others.
- Validate their feelings. Let them know you are really listening.
- Remind them that Jesus is with them and provides comfort and peace.
- Direct them to God's Word using one of the Bible passages listed in this chapter.

JOURNAL PROMPT:

How can you be intentional? How can you change your ways?

MYTH 2
IT ALL STARTS WITH ME

"Success is not given; it's earned."

"Self-belief will always give you success."

"Success doesn't come to you; you go to it."

"Work for it more than you hope for it."

"If my mind can conceive it, I can achieve it."

Ahh . . . success . . . the goal everyone strives for. We live in a society that values winning, wealth, fancy clothes, and bathtubs full of money. We may have been born into wealthy families, and we are told to continue that trajectory. Some of us may have been pushed to work hard and gain success to help our families out of poverty. Many of us are somewhere in the middle.

No matter where we started, according to the Western world, wealth (and abundant wealth at that) is where happiness resides. If we don't have it, we are not truly happy, right? If you can't afford the latest iPhone, the spring break trip to Mexico, or to have your kids in the best of the best, you're not doing it right. Right?

So, we strive daily to hit the benchmark of success. We strive for perfection. We strive for what we are told to believe will make us accepted in today's culture. Along the way, we hear phrases that fill our flesh and ego and do not lead us toward the kingdom of God and what He promises to us.

I heard this type of message for the first time at a personal development conference. As someone who always wants to grow her mind, I was looking forward to this event, and while I learned so much, this message left me confused and inspired a deep theology talk with my

MYTH 2: IT ALL STARTS WITH ME

husband. Welcome to the Doerr household. If we are confused, we talk and ask questions. We dive into the Scriptures, potentially consulting others and our pastor. And then we talk some more.

During this conference, a speaker said, "If you want it badly enough, you will be successful. You're not successful because you don't want it bad enough." That is just the perfect sound bite, the perfect clip to blast all over social media. It gets people cheering and jumping up and down and fills your flesh with the warm fuzzy it craves. If someone has ever told you something like "Success comes to those who work for it" or "If my mind can conceive it, I can achieve it," you may have felt this same fleshly desire too. It truly is a surface-level, feel-good, gets-you-fired-up phrase. And it's exactly what that personal development conference promised would happen.

A deeper dive prompts this question: Do these words really get us fired up to reach our goals? And what are those goals? God and His will for us, or us and our capabilities? Cheering, jumping, and high-fiving aside, what success are we looking for?

I left that session wondering, *What does "badly enough" mean? How do you quantify that? Is it working until you can't sleep and you've created insomnia for yourself? Is it pleading with God, on your knees, in prayer every day and night? Is it neglecting your health, your family, and your other obligations because caring for them would show you don't care enough about success?*

Confused and questioning what success truly means, I asked my husband, "So, if we work hard, our success will come to us. If we just do the steps, it'll happen. Right?" My sweet husband shrugged his shoulders and said, "If it's according to God's will, we can achieve that, but God doesn't have to bless hard work and goal-setting by answering our prayers the way we want them to be answered."

Insert my ugh-you-are-a-buzzkill face.

Now, that's not the answer that gets people cheering and makes them feel all inspired and warm and fuzzy. It's the reality that leaves people frustrated and slightly annoyed when truth breaks their

I-can-do-whatever-I-want-if-I-just-believe-in-myself bubble. I confess that I want to live in that bubble. I, too, can feel annoyed when Preston (or anyone else) reminds me where success comes from. This also helps me see that what I view as success may not be according to God's purposes for my life.

We see this unfold with the Israelites in Deuteronomy 8:11–15:

> Take care, lest you forget the LORD your God by not keeping His commandments and His rules and His statutes, which I command you today, lest, when you have eaten and are full and have built good houses and live in them, and when your herds and flocks multiply and your silver and gold is multiplied and all that you have is multiplied, then your heart be lifted up, and you forget the LORD your God, who brought you out of the land of Egypt, out of the house of slavery, who led you through the great and terrifying wilderness, with its fiery serpents and scorpions and thirsty ground where there was no water, who brought you water out of the flinty rock, who fed you in the wilderness with manna that your fathers did not know, that He might humble you and test you, to do you good in the end.

The Israelites repeatedly forgot all that God had done for them. God took them out of slavery, fed them, clothed them, gave them water, protected them, and multiplied their wealth. Yet they still were tempted and believed in their hearts that they did all of those things, not God.

Whenever I read about the Israelites, I think, *How could they forget so easily?* I mean, God sent them manna and quail every day. He gave them water and protected them. He didn't even let their clothes or their shoes wear out. Forty years isn't really a long time. God's provision was visible to them every day—so how could they forget about it?

But when I think about God's gifts to me every day, I realize that forgetting about all He does is actually pretty easy.

Recently, my husband was promoted to assistant principal. When we heard the news, I immediately said, "Congrats, Preston! Look at what those years of servant leadership, master classes, and bettering yourself have gotten you." While all of this is true, I had forgotten the most important part. It's a "Yes, and . . ." moment. Yes, Preston did all

MYTH 2: IT ALL STARTS WITH ME

of those things, and he did them well, hence the promotion, and God equipped him. God gave him the gifts of leadership and being relational with people. God placed him at this school at this time. The Holy Spirit worked through his education and experience to help him in this professional journey. God allowed the doors to be open at his current school so we could stay close to our family and continue being a part of a school environment that has become a family. God did that, not Preston.

I look at my own journey with anxiety and therapy and think about how well I can handle moments that would have previously caused my anxiety to intensify and caused an attack. While I'm still anxious, I have more control and ease of mind. But is that me or is that God working through the tools I've learned in therapy? Therapy has taught me how to breathe properly and how to ground my thoughts. I believe that God equipped my therapist with the knowledge and tools needed to teach me how to cope. It's clear to me that God opened my mind and ears to the thought of therapy and to drop the misconception that accepting help is weak.

It can be easy for me to just sit back and proudly congratulate myself by saying "Look at all my hard work." After all, I did the work. I attended the sessions, kept a journal, and tried again and again to apply the techniques to situations that cause me the most anxiety. However, none of that is possible without the Holy Spirit working in me and through others.

Matthew 7:7 says, "Ask, and it will be given to you; seek, and you will find; knock, and it will be opened to you." This verse is often used to affirm the phrases surrounding believe it, pray it, hope for it, and so on. We start to believe that if we do x, we will be rewarded with y. There is ample proof of earthly success as a reward for temporal hard work. And there is ample proof of hard work not paying off. But if your definition of success is eternal life with Jesus, you can't do x to get Jesus' y. His work on the cross is the y—His love for us earned our forgiveness, grace, and eternity with Him.

In Matthew 7:7, Jesus told the disciples to pray boldly. Like any loving Father, God will hear and answer our prayers according to His purposes—according to what He determines is best for His children. But isn't it just like sinful humans to take the first part of that verse and ignore the second? At least I find myself doing that. We hear the words "God will hear and answer our prayers, so pray boldly." We pray continually, we ask others to pray on our behalf, we send out pleas via social media for people who don't know us to pray and pray boldly. So what happens when God doesn't answer our prayers the way we want Him to? I mean, He *did* hear the prayers; we know He did.

We prayed for a way to move closer to our family, but we didn't pray to get laid off from that conveniently located job.

We prayed for help communicating better with our spouse, but we didn't pray for our communication skills to be sharpened by more disagreements.

We prayed for children, but we didn't pray for illnesses and discipline problems.

I prayed for my cousin to be found healthy and safe after going missing; I didn't pray for her to be in heaven with Jesus at the age of 24 (where she is, truly healthy and safe).

We find ourselves like David in Psalm 22:1–2:

> My God, my God, why have You forsaken me? Why are You so far from saving me, from the words of my groaning? O my God, I cry by day, but You do not answer, and by night, but I find no rest.

We keep thinking that God is completely ignoring our prayers. We know He can hear us, and knowing that definitely makes it feel worse when He doesn't appear to be answering the way we want Him to. We feel abandoned and left out in the cold. I believe that's why the word *forsaken* is so powerful here. David recited it, and so did Jesus on the cross during His crucifixion.

> And about the ninth hour Jesus cried out with a loud voice, saying, "Eli, Eli, lema sabachthani?" that is, "My God, My God, why have You forsaken Me?" (Matthew 27:46)

Let's consider this for a moment. Jesus—both Son of man and Son of God—was forsaken. He was deserted, abandoned by His Father. He died alone. He suffered hell alone.

MYTH 2: IT ALL STARTS WITH ME

I joke with friends that, when I arrive in heaven, Jesus and I will sit, sip a cup of heavenly coffee, and talk about everything I've ever wondered about while on this earth. One of the first things I might say is, "Tell me about being forsaken by God."

We'll never know what that was like. Jesus was forsaken because He took on our punishment. He took on the wrath of God for all the sins of all the world. Part of that wrath included complete and utter separation from God. Jesus did this so we could be reconciled to God and have eternal life with Him in heaven, so we would never be separated from our heavenly Father.

We are continually told by secular self-help books, motivational speakers, throw pillows at the home decor store, and society as a whole that if we just keep praying, just keep believing, all of our wildest dreams will come true. Every. Single. One. This worldly message insists that we dictate our success. We can do it! If it is to be, it's up to me! God is just the fancy Guy we thank at our acceptance speech after hearing all the accolades for all the things we did to get there. Right?

Yet is that what is promised to us? I've read the Bible and have yet to find any verse that says, "All of your dreams, they will all come true, exactly how you want them to, in the exact time frame you want. Just pray a little harder. Believe in yourself."

No, the Bible doesn't say anything like that. And I don't want to set up this chapter as "I can't pray to God about everything, and He will not bless my prayers." On the contrary. The Creator of the universe definitely can do anything. He can heal us in an instant. He can wipe away every tear and every pain. John reminds us of this promise in Revelation 21:4:

He will wipe away every tear from their eyes, and death shall be no more, neither shall there be mourning, nor crying, nor pain anymore, for the former things have passed away.

He hears every prayer in Jesus' name because Jesus is the way to the Father. Be assured that God can and will heal us, completely, when Jesus returns.

What I want to point out and help us to consider is when we pray, when we ask these things about our success and our wealth, where do we believe help comes from? We say we are #blessed, but in the thick of our successes and answered prayers, do we truly believe God the Father has blessed us, or do we believe we did it all and tack on His name as an afterthought? Does our humble bragging get more street cred by pulling out His name to fellow believers?

Again, that's not what our flesh and ego want to hear. When we walk on this road of earthly success and believe that all good things come from us and not from God, we are marching farther and farther away from Christ. We are reminded of this in James 1:17:

> **Every good gift and every perfect gift is from above, coming down from the Father of lights, with whom there is no variation or shadow due to change.**

Let us look further in the book of James. It is believed that Jesus' brother James wrote this book. In the verses preceding verse 17, James reminds us that the love of wealth and trusting in our own earthly strength and desires can lead us to fall away from Christ. James tells us to specifically pray for wisdom and have faith in God. Yet when we doubt that God can provide all things for us and believe instead that our success falls on us, we are on shaky ground:

> **For that person must not suppose that he will receive anything from the Lord; he is a double-minded man, unstable in all his ways.**
> (James 1:7)

He continues this lesson by comparing brothers, one who is humble and one who is arrogant. While success and wealth can bring many accomplishments, we can be tempted to believe we did it all on our own and trust ourselves instead of God and His provision. When we put our trust in ourselves, we risk making ourselves idols. The question then is, Where does our faith truly reside?

THE RICH YOUNG MAN

Jesus warns us of this temptation and downfall in Matthew 19:23–24:

> **And Jesus said to His disciples, "Truly, I say to you, only with difficulty**

will a rich person enter the kingdom of heaven. Again I tell you, it is easier for a camel to go through the eye of a needle than for a rich person to enter the kingdom of God."

How's that for imagery? Now, where some Christians take this verse is straight to "If you have success and wealth, you will not enter the kingdom of God," to which I politely rebuke you. This is where the context of Bible verses matters, and it matters a lot.

A rich young man approached Jesus and asked, "Teacher, what good deed must I do to have eternal life?" (Matthew 19:16). Right here, we see how this man viewed eternal life. *Good deed.* The perfectionist and rule-follower in me feels this man's pain. What steps, exactly, do I need to do, to perfection, to get what I truly want? This man believed that in order to spend eternity with Jesus, he would need to perfectly fulfill God's Law.

In true Jesus fashion, the Teacher responded by pointing away from this young man's accomplishments and wealth and toward God. "Why do you ask Me about what is good? There is only one who is good" (v. 17). Jesus then challenged him by telling him to keep all the Commandments. The young man believed he had kept them all, for he answered boldly: "All these I have kept. What do I still lack?" (v. 20).

Can we pause? I wonder what the disciples' faces looked like, what they were thinking. They heard Jesus teaching the Scriptures, witnessed His divinity as He performed miracles, and watched as more and more came to Him. They knew firsthand that Jesus spoke with the authority of God. The Bible doesn't reveal how the disciples responded, but we can imagine how we would. Haven't we gone to God with that same attitude? "Lord, I didn't do that. It was their fault. I did everything perfectly. Everyone makes mistakes." And so on.

It was truly a moment of conviction for this young man as Jesus got to the main point of how completely perfect we have to be to be able to enter the kingdom of heaven on our own efforts.

> Jesus said to him, "If you would be perfect, go, sell what you possess and give to the poor, and you will have treasure in heaven; and come, follow Me." When the young man heard this he went away

sorrowful, for he had great possessions." (Matthew 19:21–22)

The rich young man said he kept all the commandments, yet did he? Or did he actually break the first one (Love your God above all else)? We find at the end of verse 22 that he loved his possessions more than Jesus, for when asked to give them up, he walked away. It is not wealth and success that make it difficult to get into heaven; it is the love of those things that does.

This account warns us of what loving wealth and our accomplishments more than the Lord can do to us. It can make us believe that we are perfect (he said he never broke a commandment) and that our possessions are worth more than walking with Jesus.

May we keep the love of God at the forefront of our lives. May we remember that our blessings come from Him and Him alone. We can use the First Commandment to help keep our hearts aligned with what God commands of us: "You shall have no other gods before Me" (Exodus 20:3). We can remind ourselves that a "god" can be money, sex, work, our job, ourselves, success itself, and so on.

ZACCHAEUS

I once took my students on a field trip to Lauritzen Gardens, a beautiful place in Omaha, Nebraska, sectioned into different types of gardens. It's quaint, scenic, and makes you forget that you're on the edge of a major city. I find its flowers, trees, water features, and paths to be peaceful and calming. Our tour guide that day took us past a sycamore tree. Knowing that our class is from a Lutheran private school, she asked if we knew the song about Zacchaeus. Many started singing this classic Sunday School song, a few at the top of their lungs, for everyone around to hear the story of Zacchaeus.

You'll recall that Zacchaeus was a tax collector, and he was rich. In Jesus' day, he wasn't well-liked. Honestly, in today's world, he may not be well-liked. Zacchaeus used his position for his own gain and wealth. He had become lost. But on the day Luke writes about, he wanted to see Jesus, and there Jesus met him, calling out, "Zacchaeus, hurry and come down, for I must stay at your house today" (Luke 19:5).

MYTH 2: IT ALL STARTS WITH ME

The difference between the young man in Matthew and Zacchaeus in Luke is that when Jesus confronted them, one walked away in sorrow and kept his wealth, while the other gave away half of his possessions and met Jesus joyfully. One stayed in sin, and one repented. One kept his faith in his possessions, and one put his faith in Jesus. I pray that we can be like Zacchaeus, that we can repent of our sins and put our faith in Jesus, instead of looking to our earthly possessions and our own flesh.

CAN PEOPLE OF WEALTH BENEFIT THE KINGDOM?

Let's look at another person of wealth: Lydia (my favorite Bible account and namesake of my firstborn). We turn to Acts 16:11–15. Paul traveled to Philippi and met Lydia, a Gentile. Lydia was "a seller of purple goods" (v. 14). This was an expensive and famous dye and was a very profitable trade. Lydia would work with wealthy people as her clientele. In today's world, she could be the one dressing celebrities and politicians. She likely was an in-demand businesswoman.

The Holy Spirit worked through Paul to turn Lydia's heart toward Christ. We learn that she and her entire household were baptized and followed Christ (v. 15). She then welcomed Paul into her home to come and stay (v. 15). Many believe that her home became the headquarters for their mission work in Philippi. She used her wealth and status among the Philippians to spread the Gospel.

So often when we hear of women in the Bible, we hear of Martha preparing the food and the Samaritan woman at the well gathering water. Although Luke mentions several women who followed Jesus, rarely do we hear of the women who helped run and support the Gospel mission. Yet as this account indicates, Lydia was a woman of means and influence. Her position, with the Holy Spirit working through her, contributed to the success of Paul's missionary work in Philippi.

I think of the business contacts she may have had and the people she was friends with and may have witnessed to. Did she introduce Paul to the wealthy men and women of the city? Did they believe and use their own influence for Christ? While that's a question for heaven, I can't help but ponder the impact Lydia had on the spreading of the Gospel.

GOD'S ENCOURAGING WORD

IT STARTS AND ENDS WITH GOD'S STRENGTH

Lastly, we can look at one of the most famous people in the Bible that God used: David. A literal king, the epitome of wealth during that day, David's work in God's kingdom was profound. Before we dive into his reign, let's find him in one of the most well-known Bible accounts, the one with Goliath.

To recap, the Philistines were trying to fight the Israelites. They had a giant, a champion called Goliath of Gath. He was so renowned for his strength that no one from the Israelite army would go up against him. The Holy Spirit brought anger into David as he questioned the men near him: "Who is this uncircumcised Philistine, that he should defy the armies of the living God?" (1 Samuel 17:26). David was still too young to serve in Israel's army (he was there bringing supplies for his three oldest brothers), yet the Holy Spirit moved his heart to bring forth anger and encourage him to step up and fight.

David went to Saul and told him that he would fight. Saul didn't think he could do it, yet David responded with not what he had done but what God had done for him while he was a shepherd guarding his flock. David reminded Saul that God delivered him then and He would deliver him now against the Philistine (see 1 Samuel 17:37).

David didn't use Saul's armor or any weapons that were customary at that time. I'm sure I would be thinking the same that others around him may have thought: "What in the world are you doing? No armor. No weapon, but a sling and rock. This kid is crazy." David called this out as he approached the Philistine: "I come to you in the name of the LORD of hosts, the God of the armies of Israel, whom you have defied" (1 Samuel 17:45).

The account of David and Goliath is a reminder to all of us that the most advanced protections and weapons of this world do not protect us and deliver us from evil. No, it is God. It is His power and strength that helps us. It's a reminder that when all seems impossible, God's strength is shown in our weakness. This account starts with the Holy Spirit moving in David's heart to voice his conviction to Saul and ends with God's strength delivering the Israelites from the Philistines.

MYTH 2: IT ALL STARTS WITH ME

WHO ARE WE WITHOUT JESUS?

Let's take a look at 1 Samuel 16:1. God rejected Saul as Israel's king because of his disobedience. He sent the prophet Samuel to Jesse of Bethlehem to anoint a new king that God chose. Here is another reminder that our success does not come from us but from God. David would have never been contended against Saul to be king, but God chose him and made him the king over all Israel. Anointed as Israel's king and filled with the Holy Spirit, David then went out with a stone and sling and slew Israel's enemy.

After Saul died in battle, David became king over all Israel. David continued to rule and "became greater and greater, for the LORD, the God of hosts, was with him" (2 Samuel 5:10). David continued to grow in power and knew where all of his success came from. "And David knew that the LORD had established him king over Israel, and that He had exalted his kingdom for the sake of His people Israel" (2 Samuel 5:12).

David used his influence to acquire wealth and political and military power. Powerful and mighty, he united the lands of the twelve tribes and ruled over a vast area. Such a powerful leader also acquires enemies. Throughout his rule, other nations tried to defeat him. But again, with God's favor and after praying to the Lord, David knew he would win (see vv. 17–21).

God sometimes uses earthly power and wealth to further His kingdom. Where things go wrong is when we replace "God" with "I" and forget who truly is giving us these incredible blessings. You see, David knew that God was the one providing these blessings. He "knew that the LORD had established him" (v. 12). He consulted God when he heard of new enemies. He danced, feasted, and worshiped "before the LORD" (2 Samuel 6:17–19).

I find David's prayer of gratitude to be a great reminder of the blessings that God has placed upon us. Follow me to 2 Samuel 7:18. Verses 18–29 are an entire prayer, but this first line, verse 18, is one I often reference:

GOD'S ENCOURAGING WORD

> Who am I, O Lord GOD, and what is my house that You have brought me thus far?

Who are we? Who are we without God, our Father? What kind of businessman or businesswoman are we? What kind of teacher, parent, sibling, or child are we if we don't have God and His Son, Jesus, to lean on and build our foundation upon? Are we faster to anger? Are we more lost? Do we struggle more with forgiveness?

Thinking about what life looks like without Jesus is a thought that gets real dark real quick. These questions remind me of a funeral I attended for a person who was not a believer. As a lifelong Christian, with a lot of my circle and family also Christians, it was the only funeral I've attended that was not held in a church.

This person had "everything"—a loving family, a group of fun friends, and a well-paying job that person seemed to love. As I drove to the funeral, I kept thinking, "What will they talk about?" I couldn't wrap my mind around a funeral that didn't speak of heaven and the Good News of Jesus. As I walked into that funeral home, I felt an unfamiliar despair. Maybe you've been to a funeral like this too. People of course were sad about the departure of this loved one, but there was no lightness. It was just heavy. When we don't have Jesus, there is a void and a despair that are heart-wrenching.

SOCIAL MEDIA REMINDER

Currently, I am sitting in my favorite coffee shop. It's playing Christian music, and people are bustling about, working on their projects, or enjoying conversations with friends. It's become one of my favorite places away from home. As I sit, I decide to hop on social media to take a break from writing. (I'm sure you understand.) I'm ready for the photo of my cute nieces or the latest antics of my friend's dog.

As I scroll, I spot a quote someone posted from an anonymous source that made me chuckle aloud. God truly can use anything to get a point across, can't He? The quote stated this:

MYTH 2: IT ALL STARTS WITH ME

I was looking for someone to inspire me, motivate me, support me, keep me focused. Someone who would love me, cherish me, and I realized all along that I was looking for myself.

There we go, folks. I hope you chuckled just like I did. As I read the quote, I wondered, *Where is Jesus?* Although it made me laugh, it made me sad at the same time. For me, Jesus inspires me, motivates me, supports me, and keeps me focused on the kingdom of God and His will for my life. Jesus loves me and cherishes me. And I don't have to find Him because He found me. He sought me. He gives me all these things, and so much more, without measure.

We can get caught up in ourselves, and our inner sinner can believe it all has to do with what we do. That's putting unnecessary stress on ourselves because it is Jesus and His Holy Spirit working through us who accomplish these things for us.

Let's focus on Paul's first letter to the Corinthians:

So whether you eat or drink, or whatever you do, do all to the glory of God. (1 Corinthians 10:31)

While this verse speaks to the point of eating food sacrificed to idols, the words "Do all to the glory of God" are some we can lean on time and time again. When we are working toward our goals, climbing the ladder at work, or serving in our vocations as parent and spouse, may we give the glory to God. May we not boast of our own doing and how well we handle our commitments or how hard we work but of how the Holy Spirit works through us, using our spiritual gifts, to glorify God and be a witness for Him and the work He has done in us and through us to better His kingdom.

PRAYER:

Lord God,
Thank You for blessing our family with opportunity, providing for their daily needs, and using the Holy Spirit to work through us to bless others. Forgive us for getting caught up in the symbols and status of this world and forgetting where our true wealth comes from. May we use our blessings to further Your kingdom according to Your will.
In Jesus' name. Amen.

GENTLE REMINDERS:

- Success is not a sin; the love of money and success over the love of God is sinful.

- Express gratitude, daily, to God for the blessings in your life. This can look like actions from saying one thing you're thankful for as you brush your teeth in the morning to writing what you're grateful for in your journal at night.

JOURNAL PROMPT:

Where does your ego come in? How could you remove your ego and let God in?

MYTH 3
I AM STRONGER THAN MY OBSTACLES

"I am stronger than _____."

"I overcame my obstacles."

"My strength comes from within me."

"God helps those who help themselves."

When I was growing up and while I was in college, I believed this phrase: "I can overcome anything set before me." I was diagnosed with generalized anxiety disorder when I was fifteen, so this phrase made me believe I could be stronger than my mental illness. I mean, "Just don't worry," right? Man, if only it was that simple of a solution. For those of you reading who have anxiety, I hope you laughed a little. We know that anxiety can be so much more than a simple "worry" that we can willfully overcome.

For a long time, I was anxious while driving during bad weather. Yes, I'm from Nebraska. Winter gets bad here. I "should" know how to drive in it. But I didn't.

The panic would rise every time bad weather was happening. Sweaty palms, shaking, crying, heavy breathing. None of these physical symptoms made my driving any better. After a particular rainstorm induced a panic attack that left me defeated and exhausted and unable to walk into the building where I work, I knew I needed to get help. I started to attend therapy. (Side note: Book that therapy appointment. You'll be glad you did. Know this for certain: the Holy Spirit equips and calls people to work in this field and works through them to help us navigate this world.)

In therapy, I learned about grounding. According to the University of New Hampshire, grounding is a technique that helps to reorient you to the here and now of reality. You can "ground yourself" by finding things based on your senses, such as, "What do you see? What do you hear? What do you smell?"[1] I learned how to make deep breathing such a practice that it has become second nature. These tools benefit me, and I'm so thankful for them. So much so that I began to view them and my strength as the reason I was getting better. I truly believed *I* was the one who was handling my panic attacks. *I* was keeping my cool by doing the deep breathing techniques to drive through bad weather. It was me and solely me.

So what happened when I didn't handle a situation with ease? What happened when I couldn't calm my breathing and needed help from my husband to ride out the attack? I felt like a failure. I felt shame. How could I let this happen? My perfectionist self came in full force, and I believed I wasn't strong enough. How could I be so weak? I must do better, put in more work, so that one day I *will* be strong enough.

Looking back, I wish I could hug that girl. I wish I could tell her that she wasn't alone during those times of panic and anxiousness. I wish I could tell her that Jesus was right beside her. He was equipping her with the people and the behavior tools she needed; He was giving her the strength to either withstand an attack or curb it altogether. It was Jesus, not her, bringing her healing.

GOD CARES FOR YOU

We will encounter many struggles in this world. Some of those struggles come daily, like the ones we endure in the carpool lane, at the grocery store, or during nightly family routines. When we think of our daily needs, we often fall back on our own efforts. The worrying part of my brain gets a lot more use now that I'm a mother than it used to. Is the food I buy and prepare healthy enough; are there hidden dangers in every bite? Do I keep the house clean enough? Are my kids developmentally on track? Are they getting enough sleep?

Maybe you've had these same thoughts, or maybe your day-to-day concerns are different. Maybe your thoughts are *Is my child doing okay*

MYTH 3: I AM STRONGER THAN MY OBSTACLES

at college? Will this be the doctor appointment that brings happy news? Can I find a new job soon to help household finances? How's my mother coping with the loss of my dad?

These are all common worries during any moment of the day. In these moments, we can lean on our own understanding and our own power—or we can lean on Jesus and His strength. One will leave us feeling just as worried and maybe even more so; the other can leave us safe and hopeful for things to come.

I think of the account of Jesus feeding the five thousand. A basic need for all people is food. For many of us, that's not something we worry about. It's more of a concern about what to plan for supper than a worry about having nothing to feed our children. This truly is an apples to oranges comparison. When we read the account of the feeding of the five thousand, we see that Jesus asked, "Where are we to buy bread, so that these people may eat?" (John 6:5). Jesus used this question to test the disciples. He wanted their faith to be strengthened at a time when there didn't seem to be an answer. How could these thirteen men (Jesus and the Twelve) feed five thousand people with no marketplace and, if there was a marketplace, no money? Jesus knew. He wanted them to know too. Jesus used a worry and a concern to show them that He meets our real needs. We can lean on Him to provide for us.

Now, the point of this miracle is not that Jesus might come into your house tonight and help you cook your supper. Although He could, and that would be awesome, and the stories told around the table would be awe-inspiring.

Instead, the part of this biblical account that can apply to our own story is this: When we are hit with a situation, a worry, or a concern that we are struggling with and we are not sure what to do, we can turn to Jesus. We can remind ourselves that Jesus is using every circumstance to strengthen our confidence in Him. We can rely on His strength and wisdom in our lives and His provision for us, not our own.

There are many accounts in the Bible where God strengthens His people by providing for their everyday needs. For example, look again at the delivery of manna to the Israelites each morning. The central theme of this account is one we can remember in our own lives. We find the Israelites wandering the wilderness in Exodus 16. They said,

> **Would that we had died by the hand of the Lord in the land of Egypt, when we sat by the meat pots and ate bread to the full, for you have brought us out into this wilderness to kill this whole assembly with hunger.** (Exodus 16:3)

The Israelites were struggling with the basic need of hunger. One of the things I love about this story is how God responded through Moses. Friend, God didn't hear their cries and go, "People, you're being dramatic. You literally just got saved from slavery. Be thankful and deal with it." God didn't say, "Go figure it out yourself." He didn't respond with insensitivity and invalidation.

No! God responded with, "Behold, I am about to rain bread from the heaven for you" (Exodus 16:4). Moses went on to say,

> **At evening you shall know that it was the Lord who brought you out of the land of Egypt, and in the morning you shall see the glory of the Lord, because He has heard your grumbling against the Lord. For what are we, that you grumble against us?** (Exodus 16:6–7)

Moses then stated, "What are we? Your grumbling is not against us but against the Lord" (Exodus 16:8). Moses told the Israelites that their grumbling was a sin. They were going against God. And in the middle of their sin, God still provided for them. He still gave them food.

Every year, when I read this account with my class of first graders from a children's Bible, we say a phrase after almost every paragraph. That phrase is "God cares for you." Friend, we are going to sin. We are going to grumble day in and day out. (Man, I've already grumbled a lot this morning, and it's not even 9:00 a.m.) You too, or just me? We grumble in the car about the traffic. We grumble at our children when they act like getting out the door in the morning is a competition to see who can be the slowest. We grumble in our vocations when deadlines are looming or coworkers are causing us to fret and question ourselves.

We are grumblers, just like the Israelites. Yet in the middle of our sin, God still cares for us. God still provides for us and considers us His children.

MYTH 3: I AM STRONGER THAN MY OBSTACLES

ARE WE GRUMBLING OR CASTING OUR ANXIETIES ON HIM?

This is a good time to discuss what is grumbling and what is us going to God with our petitions and confessing to Him what is on our hearts. Let's look at what these words mean. The word *grumble* means "to mutter in discontent." We know we will have moments of discontentment. We can have them morning, noon, or night. Our fleshly desire will always lead us to discontentment. Have you had moments of discontentment? Have you muttered under your breath before? I have to chuckle because twelve-year-old Faith was the queen of muttering under her breath. My mother can readily vouch for that. Obviously, I knew way more than my parents. (Didn't you at that age?)

We will have moments just like the Israelites when we forget the power and glory of our God. I mean, they literally forgot that God took them out of Egypt, helped them cross the Red Sea, and was leading them with clear directions (a pillar of fire at night and a pillar of cloud during the day) (see Exodus 14). It didn't take long for them to start muttering. On the fifteenth day of the second month after they left Egypt, about six weeks of freedom from slavery, they started to grumble (see Exodus 16:1).

Are you like that? God answers your prayers, but you respond with more complaints? Did He open an opportunity for you to provide for your family but you quickly saw a flaw in that opportunity? You saw His hand at work in your life, but after a few days or weeks, that work isn't exactly what you want?

Honestly, I do this. An example of God answering a prayer and me responding with a grumble is when my husband and I prayed for a baby. We wanted to start our family. One afternoon, while my husband was playing in his golf league, I took three pregnancy tests. Yes, three. Three can't lie, right? I was so excited that I created a scavenger hunt for him to find the tests. (Yes, I can be that person when I want to be.) I sat, with excitement and jitters, waiting for him to come home. I kept thinking, "Will he be speechless? Will he cry? Will he jump up and down and scream like he does at football games?"

Friend, I can laugh at myself now, but when he came home, he did not give me an enthusiastic response to my seek-and-find game. No. My husband walked in the door and said, "Played the worst round of my life." He was in full grumble mode. If you play golf or have a loved one who does, then I know you know what he was feeling. Here is where I turned my answered prayer into my own grumble mode. "How can he be upset? Doesn't he see I'm wanting to talk to him about something? Can't he see my excitement?"

Disclaimer: Communication matters, and this would have been a great time to exercise that muscle of healthy communication. God didn't give my husband mind-reading capabilities. And I didn't communicate to him what I was feeling. Instead, I grumbled that my reveal didn't go the way I wanted it to go.

Choosing between grumbling and going to God with our frustrations and disappointments is intentional. When we grumble, we are thinking through the lens of "woe is me." Our sinful flesh defaults into self-centered grumbling. If we are not intentional about how we voice our expectations, we fall into that trap.

When my husband didn't come home ready to recognize my mood and partake in my fun scavenger hunt, I had a pity party. I focused inward. My expectations weren't met. And I was as blind to my husband's mood in the moment as he was to mine.

If grumbling is self-focused discontentment, what does casting our cares on God mean? Casting is to toss out. We are to cast out our ego-centric self-pity and instead look to God's guidance and wisdom to put our concerns into a larger perspective.

The word *casting* calls to mind fishing. Fishermen will tell you there is a lot of intentionality when it comes to this pastime. You need a rod, a line, bait or a lure, and a type of fish you hope to attract. When you cast, you don't cast a foot or so in front of you. Rather, you set your sights on a point out far into the water to cast your line out there.

We do the same when we go to God with our concerns. As Peter indicated in 1 Peter 5:7, "Casting all your anxieties on Him, because He cares

MYTH 3: I AM STRONGER THAN MY OBSTACLES

for you," when we cast our cares, we throw them far away from us. We don't drop them right in front of us where we can easily pick them up again. We send them away for God to pick up.

Psalm 55:22 states, "Cast your burden on the Lord, and He will sustain you." We don't have to hold on to our burdens; instead, we can cast them onto God and let go of them. We give them to the almighty Lord who hears us, rescues us, sustains us, and supports us. We can be intentional about this and not mindlessly reactionary.

Now that we know the difference between grumbling as our default and casting our cares as an intentional response, we can call on the Holy Spirit to change our hearts. Events in our day-to-day lives may cause us to wonder why—why do we try? Why do others behave that way? Why do these things keep happening? With the Spirit's help, we can develop the habit of first remembering that God works all things for the good for those who love Him. We can ask God to guard our hearts and open our eyes to His will for us and our loved ones.

CAN WE APPLAUD HIM?

The opposite of grumbling is applauding. This antonym makes me smile because it's so true! We can sit and grumble, or we can sit and applaud. Remember that God invites us to come to Him with all things, whether our grumblings are valid or result from our misconceptions. He also gives us the Holy Spirit and the ability to change our thoughts. Research indicates that the part of the brain that holds anxiety is the same part that holds gratitude.[2] When we practice gratitude, or applause, in our daily lives, we are helping our emotional regulation lead us to good health—and the Holy Spirit is continuously transforming our hearts to fill with and reflect contentment.

If you are like me, you might get tired of people asking, "What are you thankful for today?" This question that on the surface seems to point us to thanksgiving for our God-given blessings begins to feel like Law. Nevertheless, there is power in stating what we are thankful for. As stated above, scientific research supports it. But more important,

GOD'S ENCOURAGING WORD

God tells us to do exactly that. (What an incredible thing that science is proving and giving us hard data on what God has already proclaimed.)

Friend, when we find ourselves filling up with grumbles, let us release that attitude, cast it out to God, and allow Him to soften our hearts and help us communicate in a healthy way. May we replace our grumbles with gratitude as Paul indicated. And may we look to Isaiah 26:3, "You keep him in perfect peace whose mind is stayed on You, because he trusts in You," to help us remember to set our eyes on Jesus, who is the source of our hope and strength.

WHAT DOES IT MEAN TO STRENGTHEN OUR RELATIONSHIP WITH JESUS?

So what does strengthening our relationship look like? Do we do some sort of exercise, take a quiz to clarify our thoughts? No, friend, strengthening our relationship with Jesus happens only through the work of the Holy Spirit. Turn to Philippians 4:6–7. You've heard it said once or twice and may even be able to recite it word for word:

Do not be anxious about anything, but in everything by prayer and supplication with thanksgiving let your requests be made known to God. And the peace of God, which surpasses all understanding, will guard your hearts and your minds in Christ Jesus.

Our relationship with God is strengthened when we read His words for us in the Bible, when we hear the Gospel proclaimed, and when we receive His gifts for us in the Lord's Supper. Assured that He hears our prayers, we unabashedly bring Him the things on our hearts. We turn our thoughts to God, instead of ignoring them or scrolling social media or watching the latest binge-worthy show. We let Jesus "guard [our] hearts and [our] minds."

This isn't easy. In a world that rewards snark and celebrates whining, we pick up our grumbles the moment after we give them to God in prayer. We resist change, so replacing unhealthy thoughts with healthy ones requires effort. Again, we look to God's Word for help. In Philippians 4:8–9, Paul tells us to practice thinking things that are true, honorable,

MYTH 3: I AM STRONGER THAN MY OBSTACLES

just, pure, lovely, commendable, excellent, and things worthy of praise. He knows what he's talking about. Paul was a chief persecutor of Jesus. But Jesus turned things around for Paul, for the early church—and for us.

Paul's letter to the Philippians reminds us that his situation proves God's desire to transform and strengthen us. It is because of situations he faced—plenty and hunger, abundance and need (see v. 12)—that he learned to be content and trust God's will. Those times were opportunities for him to learn to turn toward the Lord and not wallow in his discomfort.

According to a study done by the National Library of Medicine,[3] the word *resilient* can describe someone able "to bounce back from a real, experienced adversity." It's a trait, such as grit, that Angela Lee Duckworth[4] shows us that can be an indicator of success. In her TED Talk, "Grit: The Power of Passion and Perseverance," Duckworth said parents want their kids to be resilient, to develop grit in order to persevere through the challenges and milestones of life, and to develop a strong work ethic. It's a trait we all want—but how do we get it? Again, Paul shows us. Resilience is a result of putting our confidence in the God who delivered us from sin and eternal damnation. We will probably never experience the situations Paul lived through. (Thank God!) But we can know that his example is in the Bible for us to learn from.

Paul was able to face imprisonment because Jesus called him to do so. Jesus literally opened Paul's eyes to see Jesus as the Messiah. That's definitely more dire than a day of bad traffic, the meeting that feels like it will never end, or our toddlers deciding they now need to get out of bed for the tenth time instead of falling asleep. Yet even during his suffering, Paul reminds us that God works all things together for our good (see Romans 8:28).

Because Paul's writings to the early church are also for us, we can rest in knowing that in moments of disappointment and frustration, times when it seems like nothing can go right and we are at a loss, God is working for us. He is using these moments to draw us closer to Him and to our faith in His provision.

DAILY PRESSURE MAKES US WEAK. GOD MAKES US STRONG.

When I think of Paul, I think of his mission work for the Gospel and his time spent in prison. I don't think of him having daily pressure. To me, his struggles are big and mighty, not small, daily things.

In his second letter to the Corinthians, Paul recorded his many sufferings. In 2 Corinthians 11:16, for example, Paul expressed sarcasm toward the Corinthians. This part makes me chuckle. I picture the imprisoned apostle writing with a snarky tone about how the Philippians allowed Gentiles to treat them as second-class citizens. He said, "You allowed yourselves to be deceived." And he reminded them about his beatings, being stranded, being robbed, and other dangers he faced while carrying out his mission of spreading the Gospel (see vv. 21–29). Paul wrote as a servant of Christ, listing all the hardships he had to endure and how he would boast in those hardships to show that God was working in his weakness (see v. 29).

During this catalog of sufferings, he talked of the daily pressure of anxiety for all the churches he founded in his missions. The man who spent much of his ministry in prison and with his well-being threatened felt anxiety about his churches and the faith lives of the members in these churches. Paul knew—better than we do—how quickly the human heart can go from leaning on God to boasting about our own doings and about what good Christians we are. He told the Corinthians that he wanted to boast but did his best to refrain from it:

> **So to keep me from becoming conceited because of the surpassing greatness of the revelations, a thorn was given me in the flesh, a messenger of Satan to harass me, to keep me from becoming conceited.** (2 Corinthians 12:7)

God allowed him to suffer as a reminder that, in his weakness, God is strong. Jesus was too weak to carry His cross. Even though Jesus understands what it means to be weak and exhausted, He still completed our salvation.

MYTH 3: I AM STRONGER THAN MY OBSTACLES

MAY WE NOT BOAST

One of the lessons for us in Paul's account is that he didn't do this on his own. The only way he endured was by God's power. God equipped him. Paul kept this truth at the forefront of his mind and in his writings. Paul became so good at not boasting about himself that the only time he did boast, it was to emphasize his personal weakness, which revealed God's great power even more. He shows us this in 2 Corinthians 11:30:

If I must boast, I will boast of the things that show my weakness.

What a picture and way of thinking! What if the only time we boasted was to bring God even more glory? What would our social media feeds look like? What would our conversations with loved ones, and even strangers, sound like if the only time we spoke of our pressures, hardships, and annoyances was to bring glory to God and witness to His power in our daily lives?

That question truly convicts me. While I talk about showing gratitude and using our tongues for purposeful talk, I also find myself gossiping and saying unkind words. It's a habit I work on constantly, and I know God is working on me to change.

How would I feel and what would my relationships look like if every time I started to grumble, I expressed gratitude to God and His work in my daily life instead? I might sound like this:

The old me: "This traffic takes forever. I spend more time in my car than I want to. Waiting at intersections is so frustrating!"

The Spirit-led me: "I'm thankful that God has protected me and everyone else on these roads so we get to our destinations safely. Since I'm in the car so much, I have more time to pray to God with thanksgiving and giving my worries for the day to Him."

The old me: "My daughter *never* listens to me. I'm at my wits end that whenever I tell her to do something, she responds unkindly and walks away. I find myself becoming frustrated with her and end up taking it all out on her by yelling."

The Spirit-led me: "I can use this opportunity to show my child how to cope with frustration in a healthy way. I can model healthy conflict resolution strategies to strengthen our relationship as mother and daughter. And I can reinforce the God-given vocations of parent and child."

Could these moments improve the health of our relationships? Would nonbelievers wonder what was different about us, giving us an opportunity to witness to them about the love and grace of Jesus?

OUR WEAKNESS IS AN OPPORTUNITY FOR GOD

Isn't that exactly what Paul did for the majority of his missionary life? He used his own weakness to spread the Gospel. Doesn't that have more impact on our faith life?

This brings us back to the beginning of this chapter. "I overcame it on my own." "I am stronger than my obstacles." These phrases turn us completely away from God and His mighty power and toward ourselves. It takes us away from an everlasting hope and puts it into a flesh that will disappoint us 100 percent of the time.

Our flesh drags us toward gossip, lust for power, and anything sinful. Paul knew this. He knew that our sinful nature wants the opposite of what God wants for our lives. That is why he was so adamant with the Corinthians. He admonished them for focusing on their own abilities and not God's power and strength.

When we turn away from our selfish desires, with the help of God, and lean into God's strength, we become witnesses to those around us. We can be a walking testimony to contentment in God's promises. This doesn't mean we don't become frustrated, angry, or annoyed with things that happen. This does mean that we do not cave in to those feelings and allow those feelings to dictate our actions. Paul reminds us that our strength fails, but God's never will. We will have daily pressures from work, our home life, our relationships with friends, our marriage, and even our church life, but when the world encourages us to stay in the pit of complaining and grumbling, we can be a light that God is working for our good and for His purpose.

MYTH 3: I AM STRONGER THAN MY OBSTACLES

PRAYER:

Lord God,
Thank You for providing for my basic needs. Thank You for Your provision. Forgive me for when I grumble and complain instead of casting my burdens onto You. Forgive me for when I boast instead of leaning on You and Your strength. Lord, change my heart. Remind me that when I voice to You my frustrations, You will sustain me through Your Word and the Sacraments. May I lay my concerns at the cross and rest in the peace and understanding that only You provide.
In Jesus' name. Amen.

GENTLE REMINDERS:

- God cares for you and invites you to cast your burdens on Him.
- Ask the Holy Spirit to replace grumbling with gratitude.
- Use frustrations as opportunities to show God's work being done in us.
- May we not boast of our own doing but boast of God and His glory.

JOURNAL PROMPT:

What struggles cause you to grumble? How can you incorporate gratitude and praise into your daily life?

MYTH 4

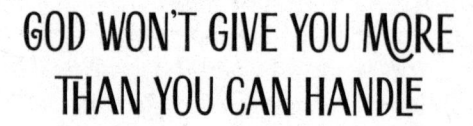

GOD WON'T GIVE YOU MORE THAN YOU CAN HANDLE

"God gives His toughest battles to His strongest soldiers."

"Only you can handle it."

"I am stronger than whatever comes my way."

Before we dive in: In the previous chapter, we talked about daily struggles like a disagreement with a coworker, the trials of parenting, or people who forget how to drive when a flake of snow hits the ground. These struggles are valid, but my therapist would give them a 2 on the 1 to 10 stress scale, with 1 at the low end of stress-inducing struggle and 10 at the high end.

What about the things on the other end of that scale—things we do not know how to recover from? This could be the death of a loved one, a divorce we didn't see coming, or the family we never had. What about then? What do we say to others when the unthinkable happens? Do we just give them a sticker that says "You've got this!" or "There, there. God won't give you anything you can't handle"?

If there was a saying I could delete from everyone's dialogue, it would be this one. Because what if we don't make it out of this? What if our prayer isn't answered the way we want? What if tackling another day is too hard? How do we get through those times?

Before I go further, I want to just let you know that I hear you. I acknowledge your pain. I recognize the dark thoughts. And I understand why you may feel that your relationship with your Savior isn't as strong as you need it to be.

MYTH 4: GOD WON'T GIVE YOU MORE THAN YOU CAN HANDLE

Life this side of heaven is *hard*. Your emotions are completely valid. At times, they're unbearable. And if you're like me, you feel despair that it has to be you or your family walking this path. Why us? Friend, if you're thinking those thoughts, please know that you are not alone. I encourage you, *plead* with you, to seek help. After my darkest moment, I scheduled a therapy appointment. It was nerve-racking. I felt that I was a failure for seeking help. But since then, I've learned that God works through therapists to bring healing and hope. If therapy isn't available, I encourage you to speak with your pastor. God has equipped him to help you navigate these times too.

This chapter is heavy. I cried a lot while writing it. Maybe my grief will always be there and I'll never be able to explain the tension that's present for me. Maybe my pain won't be healed until I get to heaven. For you, I pray that by the end of this chapter, and especially by the end of this book, you will know that you don't have to stay in this dark spot. We have a God who loves us and sent His Son, Jesus, to die for us so that these feelings of pain, these feelings of despair and desperation—they don't have to be our ending. Our present misery is caused by sin. Plain and simple. But our ending is joyful and glorious. It's filled with peace and laughter.

He will wipe away every tear from their eyes, and death shall be no more, neither shall there be mourning, nor crying, nor pain anymore, for the former things have passed away. (Revelation 21:4)

With that, let's dive deep into this myth, not looking to social media or to whatever video is online but to the true source of hope, Christ Jesus, as revealed to us in God's Word and by His Holy Spirit.

PRAY FOR PEACE AND TRUST, NOT UNDERSTANDING

I had just walked out of an exercise class. It was a forty-five-minute class where we focused on our breathing and bending our bodies to help release tension built up from the week prior. This class allowed me a time to escape the hustle of the world and to focus on breathing and praying to God. It provided me a silent place removed from the bustle outside of those walls.

Before I walked through those doors, our close-knit family was in a state of tension and chaos. My cousin had disappeared and couldn't be located. We were going on weeks by this point. Those weeks were such a blur. They say your brain blocks out traumatic events to protect itself. According to Cleveland Clinic, this is called dissociative amnesia—a state that protects your brain from trauma.[5] That's an accurate description of what I went through.

I walked out of the studio, feeling some of the tension erased, but it all came flooding back when I saw multiple missed phone calls and texts from family: "Call me." "Come to your parents' house."

I threw my mat into the backseat, started my car, and called my husband.

"Faith, come to your parents' house."

"Preston, tell me . . ."

"Not while you're driving. Hang up and come over."

I can be impatient and stubborn. I screamed over the phone for him to tell me *right now*. Tears streamed down my face and my hands shook.

It was a gut-wrenching answer I already knew in my heart but needed to hear out loud: They had found her. Well, they found her body.

She was with Jesus. I should have been rejoicing—she's with Jesus. Instead, I felt profound anger. How could this happen? Why *her*? Why our family? These are questions we didn't get answered then and never will get answered on earth.

That's exactly when the saying "God won't give you more than you can handle" became the saying I would abhor, the phrase I would forever roll my eyes at and resent hearing. I wanted to say, "How lucky are you to never have a moment you can't handle."

In true sinner form, instead of hearing those words with empathy, I was bitter.

There are things in this world that can be capital-T traumatic. Situations like assault, abuse, trafficking, murder, miscarriage, terminal illness, or accidental death. Incomprehensible things like mass shootings

MYTH 4: GOD WON'T GIVE YOU MORE THAN YOU CAN HANDLE

of children, horrific war, natural disasters. These situations cause our hearts to ache.

Yet even there, even in the cold, dark pit at the core of our pain, Jesus is there. He is there with compassion and hope and promise. He grieves with us, cries with us, holds us fast against His heart. Of this we have irrefutable proof. We can look to God's Word to see where God met others, just like us, who have been dealt hands too hard to comprehend. When we don't comprehend, we can pray, yet we don't pray for understanding. No! We pray for the peace that passes all understanding, the peace that only Jesus provides.

THE PSALMS WITH DAVID

When we think of obstacles or failing resolve, we all have a moment in our lives or that of a loved one that comes to mind. We think of the phone call about a cancer diagnosis or about someone we love in a car accident and on their way to the hospital. We think about the doctor saying the ultrasound didn't detect a heartbeat.

It's these moments—these weakening-of-the-knee moments—when we drop to the floor and think we'll never be able to get back up. This is when the Psalms help us the most. The book of Psalms is filled with an array of strong emotion, from David rejoicing to David crying out thinking the Lord has left him.

Psalm 13 especially conveys what we feel during weakening-of-the-knee moments. Like some of our prayers, the psalm starts like this:

How long, O Lord? Will You forget me forever?

How long will You hide Your face from me?

How long must I take counsel in my soul

and have sorrow in my heart all the day?

How long shall my enemy be exalted over me? (vv. 1–2)

Do you feel seen too? In the middle of sufferings, does it feel like God has left? Does it feel like He's ignoring your cries of "how long do I have to suffer"? David continues with all the wonderful things God has done for others.

Keep reading. David talks about resting in God's steadfast love. Even when he felt that God wasn't seeing him, he *still praised and loved God*! He still trusted God.

GOD CAN USE ORDINARY THINGS TO STRENGTHEN US

We can look to the account of Elijah to feel seen in our sufferings. If you follow me to 1 Kings 19, we see that Elijah is anything but happy, even after his great victory over the prophets of Baal on Mount Carmel in chapter 18. He was afraid: Jezebel had sent a messenger to Elijah telling him he was to be killed (see 1 Kings 19:2). I can only imagine all the feelings he had after receiving that threat. Did he feel shocked? persecuted? helpless? frightened? doomed? We don't know if he felt all of this, but we do know he felt afraid (see v. 3).

In his moment of fear, Elijah didn't turn to God. Instead, he ran away. He went on a day's journey into the wilderness until he found a broom tree to rest against. Then, finally, Elijah expressed himself to God. He asked God to take his life: "It is enough; now, O Lord, take away my life, for I am no better than my fathers" (v. 4). Elijah was so deep in shame and defeat when Jezebel was not brought to faith with the miracle on Mount Carmel he felt he needed to die.

(Let me interrupt here to say that if you have ever felt so hopeless that your thoughts turn to self-harm or death, please speak to someone. Call 988. Call your pastor. Call your mom or best friend or anyone you trust. Don't ignore such feelings.)

Back to Elijah. This story makes me chuckle, not because of Elijah's emotions, but because of how God responded to him. God sent an angel to comfort him and encourage him, but this angel didn't say some mighty speech or throw pixie dust on him. What did this angel say?

And behold, an angel touched him and said to him, "Arise and eat." (v. 5)

Elijah had just taken a nap. Now he was told to eat. I mean, napping and eating—it's biblical! The Saturday-morning-in-my-comfy-pajamas self loves that!

MYTH 4: GOD WON'T GIVE YOU MORE THAN YOU CAN HANDLE

This account can remind us that taking care of ourselves is important. Elijah was depleted, and God restored him. God uses ordinary things—food and sleep—that we might otherwise disregard to encourage Elijah.

What I think is interesting about this account isn't that God started with, "What are you doing?" Sure, He gets to that, but He starts with grace and provision. God's response to Elijah is supportive and encouraging. He shows Elijah mercy. A note in *The Lutheran Study Bible* quotes Martin Luther, who states it perfectly: "God wants to have patience with our weakness" (AE 5:25).

God was patient with Elijah. We can trust that God is patient with us. Friend, when we are tired, weak, and have gone too long without taking care of ourselves, God is patient with us too. This may come in the form of a friend inviting you for coffee, a glorious afternoon nap, or that encouraging hymn or worship song that comforts you. He may use things on your calendar that seem ordinary to strengthen you—choir practice, volunteer work, a visit with Grandma.

When I'm going through a tough time, I find great encouragement in a friend who invites me for coffee and spends a few hours discussing life with me. I take solace in quiet moments when I snuggle with my children. And I am comforted by the rhythms of the Divine Service, the well-known responses of the liturgy, and the handshake or hug on the way out the door toward home.

God created us to be in community, and He uses people around us to remind us that our hope is found in Jesus and the promise of eternal life. The community God creates includes Him—God the Father, the Son, and the Holy Spirit. God is our community.

If you're not going through a tough time but you know someone who is, let this be a gentle reminder to send a quick thinking-of-you text. Invite that person out for coffee, send a greeting card, or watch the baby while she takes a nap. Pray. (You don't even have to tell her that you're praying for her, but telling her will be a blessing to her.) And know that God can use any act of love to provide comfort and hope.

ARE WE ASKING THE RIGHT QUESTION?

Often in these moments of despair, I find myself thinking that God has forgotten me. I am filled with doubt, convinced God somehow just forgot to look out for me and my circumstances. As if He takes care of everyone but me. But I think I ask the wrong question. Instead of asking, "God, where did You go?" I need to ask, "God, where do I see You?"

When we are struggling with depression or depressive thoughts, thinking God has left us, we can see Him in the friend or loved one who calls to check in on us. We can see Him in the beauty of the sunrise that greets us each morning. When we are running from obligation to obligation for our children, we can see Him in the joy our child has for each activity. We can see Him in the memories created while riding in the car.

I took a doctrine class in college. It was taught by a professor who would later officiate when my husband and I got married. In class, this professor had an incredible way of helping us ask questions. For when we ask the questions, God and the Holy Spirit will lead us to the truth found in Jesus Christ's sacrifice for us.

One morning, after we shuffled into the classroom, we talked about why people have trials and tribulations. Why *do* bad things happen? It launched a serious debate during which our professor just sat there, listening intently and letting our voices be heard. It's something I admire still about him, the way he just listened. After letting the discussion go on for a while, he said one thing that had a profound impact on me: "When you find yourself in these obstacles, and you've fallen on your back, the only way you can look is up."

That one sentence has stayed with me to this day. When I am hit with trials, obstacles, and sufferings, I remind myself that God takes what is meant for evil and uses it for good. Just like Joseph said to his brothers in Genesis 50:20: "As for you, you meant evil against me, but God meant it for good, to bring it about that many people should be kept alive, as they are today." He is using it to point me back to Him, to point me back to His Son and the promise—the promise and hope that is found in Jesus and His resurrection.

MYTH 4: GOD WON'T GIVE YOU MORE THAN YOU CAN HANDLE

JOB'S FAITH

When we think of accounts of trials and obstacles in the Bible, we may think of Job first. I mean, this man is a textbook example of having bad things happen to him. Even if you know the story well, I invite you to join me in chapter 1.

We find Job sitting at the top of the world. He was upright and blameless, and he feared God (v. 1). He had ten children, a beautiful wife, and a large estate: seven thousand sheep, three thousand camels, five hundred yoke of oxen, and five hundred donkeys, along with a large number of servants (see vv. 2-3). In other words, the guy was living his best life.

Job had it all, even by today's standards. Then he lost it all. He lost *everything* (see vv. 13-19). As you read, you can feel the "and another one" "and another one" moments hitting Job. In six verses, he went from having the whole world to having nothing. What Job did next convicts me. I've lost not nearly as much as Job did, and my first reaction to my loss was not what Job's was.

In Job 1:20, we see that Job "arose and tore his robe and shaved his head and fell on the ground and worshiped." What? But ... he *worshiped*?

Maybe you're like Job. When you're hit with an unbearable event, you fall to your knees. To be honest, I didn't and sometimes still don't. I usually look up in anger and ask, "Why, God?!" This is not my finest moment, but it's also a real one. It's a sinful one, but it's also a real one.

Throughout this life, we will deal with grief, despair, and frustration. Things will happen to us, or our loved ones, and we won't understand why. Our logical brains don't know how to explain it away. These aren't moments of "Well, I didn't turn on my blinker, and I ran into a car" or "I got busy talking on the phone and burned the pie."

These are times when we did everything right but the bad thing still happened, times that you only hear about in movies and never think would happen to you or your family. Job was "blameless and upright"; even God said so (Job 1:8). Yet these awful events still happened to him. I think a lesson we can learn from Job is that we can bring God our questions, we can grieve and talk with God about our sorrow and pain, and we can know that God is with us. God will work through it, with us, not against us.

If you follow me to Job 3, we see his depression. Job no longer wanted to live. He would rather die than continue on. We see his mind had become warped with depressive thoughts. For the first time, Job held God responsible for what happened (see v. 23). He had feared losing God's favor, and at the end of this chapter, he had lost just that (see vv. 25–26). We see in chapter 7 that Job hated his life and wanted God to leave him alone: "I loathe my life; I would not live forever. Leave me alone, for my days are a breath" (v. 16).

Just like Job, we can become angry with God and even wonder if God truly loves us. When you're outside of those painful experiences, it sounds silly. But when you're in the thick of some of your darkest moments, questioning God's love is completely genuine.

Yet there is a hope we can rest in—the hope of Christ Jesus. For through Christ alone, we have confidence in God's love for us. When we struggle with these painful experiences, questioning if God is for us, we can combat those depressive thoughts with the love of Jesus. We remind ourselves of Good Friday and Easter—how God sent His one and only Son, so that whoever believes in Him will not perish but will have eternal life (see John 3:16). We must rest in the promise—not of this life but of the life to come: the promise of eternal life and happiness.

WHAT IF THE PRAYER NEVER GETS ANSWERED HOW WE WANT?

The phrases listed at the start of the chapter are ones that sound good on paper and social media but can leave us defeated in the real day-after-day struggle of dealing with it. I am reminded of my own experiences that turned this phrase on its head. You may be thinking of something in your own life too.

In moments of pure despair and exhaustion, you truly find out that phrases like "I am stronger than whatever is thrown at me today" give you nothing. They leave you with nothing, nothing of substance anyway. That phrase washed away all of its power grab on me that afternoon in

MYTH 4: GOD WON'T GIVE YOU MORE THAN YOU CAN HANDLE

December. The moments, days, and weeks after she went missing—honestly even to today—people said, "You are so strong. You are stronger than this event that happened to you. God would never have given your family this trial if He didn't think you could handle it."

By now, I'm completely annoyed and frustrated. I am not comforted. *At all*. Have you felt that same way? You've told someone, in confidence, you've miscarried for the second time this year. Your spouse has been told he has a debilitating disease, and you are now the sole caretaker. The marriage you've been working so hard for is ending, and not because you want it to.

We know people mean well when they say these things. I mean, how do you even talk to someone about this? Events like these aren't exactly addressed in our public speaking 101 class. But I couldn't handle that moment. I couldn't handle the phone call after yoga class and making my husband say what happened to my cousin out loud when I already, in my heart, knew the answer. I couldn't handle the looks on people's faces when they found out what had happened. I couldn't handle the guilt of "What if?" or the constant questions of "Why? Why our family?" I couldn't handle the investigation, the trial, and the countless news articles grasping at information that at times wasn't even true.

I COULD. NOT. HANDLE. IT.

But Jesus could, and He did.

He surrounded me with His grace and love even in times I said aloud that I didn't want Him to. (I told you I was in a bad place). God provided me with a Christian support system to ask questions of, to vent frustration to, and to just be with when I need a good ol' bear hug. And He calls to me in His Word, which is packed with reminders of His love, protection, mercy, and grace.

When we replace the phrase "I am stronger than whatever comes my way" with "Jesus is strong for me," it takes the weight off us and puts it onto Him, the one who can sustain the weight. You start to live those moments differently. It's no longer about you; it's about what Jesus is doing for you and through you.

JESUS REFINES OUR FAITH

I recently talked with a friend about some troubles she and her family were facing, about the trials of kids getting older and all that comes with having teenagers and the independence they so desperately crave. She talked about how times of frustration and struggle refine our faith and our relationship with Jesus in ways that the joyful moments never do. I couldn't help but agree with her.

When we have these moments of frustration and struggle, we can often draw away from God. We move away from Him and turn inward instead of turning outward toward Him. However, when we draw away, God draws near. In Romans 8:38–39, we are reminded that nothing can separate us from God:

> For I am sure that neither death nor life, nor angels nor rulers, nor things present, nor things to come, nor powers, nor height nor depth, nor anything else in all creation, will be able to separate us from the love of God in Christ Jesus our Lord.

David wrote Psalm 138 to give praise to God, who delivered him out of his crisis:

> **On the day I called, You answered me; my strength of soul You increased.** (v. 3)

David called out to God. God answered his prayer and gave him strength to deal with his crisis. This was not David's doing. David did nothing. God did everything. David knew that his strength was giving out and continued to call on the strength of God to support him.

> **Though I walk in the midst of trouble, You preserve my life; You stretch out Your hand against the wrath of my enemies, and Your right hand delivers me.** (Psalm 138:7)

Whatever trouble we are facing, God will preserve our lives for eternity. God's love for us will endure forever (see v. 8). We can rest with confidence that God has kept His promises in the past, and He will continue to do so, even if our present circumstances try to convince us otherwise and even if our trouble endures for the rest of our earthly lives.

MYTH 4: GOD WON'T GIVE YOU MORE THAN YOU CAN HANDLE

Paul's faith journey is another great example of how suffering can refine our faith in Christ Jesus. In his second letter to the church of Corinth, Paul compares his suffering and trials to a death sentence (see 2 Corinthians 1:9), which tells us that his sufferings were severe. Our sufferings are a result of sin entering the world. Sometimes Christians believed that your suffering meant your family had disgraced God, and He was giving in to His wrath.

I, the LORD your God, am a jealous God, visiting the iniquity of the fathers on the children to the third and fourth generation of those who hate Me, but showing steadfast love to thousands of those who love Me and keep My commandments. (Exodus 20:5-6)

Yet Paul knows and is reminding the church of Corinth that "If we are afflicted, it is for your comfort and salvation" (2 Corinthians 1:6). Paul helps us fix our eyes not on our suffering but on the "God who raises the dead" (v. 9). Our sins fell on Christ, who took them upon Himself and reconciled us to the Father through His suffering and death on the cross.

Christ redeemed us from the curse of the law by becoming a curse for us—for it is written, "Cursed is everyone who is hanged on a tree." (Galatians 3:13)

WHAT IF WE CAUSE DESTRUCTION?

If it's our fault, if the destruction is caused by something we did or didn't do, will God still work through us? While there are many things that are outside our control, there are many things within it. Because we are sinners, we often can create our own problems and turmoil. For a biblical example, look at Lot. He wouldn't be a great guy by our standards, yet God still showed him mercy.

In Genesis 19, the Lord prepared to destroy Sodom because of the wickedness that had taken root there. But first, He rescued Lot, Abraham's nephew. Two angels who looked like men arrived at Sodom and stayed with Lot. The men of Sodom, being sinful and just awful people with appalling intentions, ordered the visitors to come out (see v. 5). Lot said, "Hey, have my daughters instead." Did your skin just crawl?

(Mine did.) Second, the angels struck the men of Sodom with blindness and told Lot to leave Sodom and take his family with him. "But he lingered. So the men [angels] seized him and his wife and his two daughters by the hand, the Lord being merciful to him, and they brought him out and set him outside the city" (v. 16).

Lot callously offered to give his daughters to a gang of rapists. He dawdled at home, even after God's messengers told him explicitly to go. Lot was disobedient, but God still rescued him. God still showed mercy to him. This wild biblical account shows that even when we fall and make horrible decisions, God is still a merciful God.

The account of Samson is another Old Testament example of how we contribute to our own suffering. Samson's mother, a previously barren woman, gave birth to Samson and, at God's direction, raised him as a Nazirite: "No razor shall come upon his head, for the child shall be a Nazirite to God from the womb, and he shall begin to save Israel from the hand of the Philistines" (Judges 13:5). God gifted him with incredible strength for the purpose of destroying Israel's enemy, the Philistines.

Young, impulsive, and arrogant, Samson was known then and now for his incredible strength. He was not known for making thoughtful choices. Samson pushed for an inappropriate, illegal marriage to a Philistine woman (see Judges 14:3). He made a bet with his Philistine groomsmen and lost. To meet the terms of the bet, he slaughtered other Philistines and plundered their goods. In the meantime, his father-in-law promised his bride to a Philistine man, and Samson retaliated by burning the fields of the Philistines. The Philistines retaliated against Samson by burning the father-in-law's house with the father-in-law and Samson's bride inside. This back-and-forth destruction continued.

Samson's biography includes other licentious and violent behaviors, but despite his sinfulness, "the Spirit of the Lord rushed upon him" (Judges 14:19) to do the work of God. Samson went against God's will when he got with Delilah and ended up telling her the secret of where his strength lay (see Judges 16:17). Betrayed by Delilah, defeated by the Philistines, blinded, and imprisoned, Samson eventually figured things out.

MYTH 4: GOD WON'T GIVE YOU MORE THAN YOU CAN HANDLE

When we despair of ourselves and our own wrongdoings, God uses it as an opportunity to call us to go to Him for strength. After being defeated, Samson called upon the Lord: "O Lord God, please remember me and please strengthen me only this once, O God, that I may be avenged on the Philistines for my two eyes" (Judges 16:28). In his death, Samson destroyed the government of Philistia. Samson caused much of his own despair, but God still worked through him. Just like Samson, we can repent of our sins and call on God to help us. We can ask God to change our hearts and accomplish His will for the good of His kingdom.

In the accounts of both Lot and Samson, we are shown that there will be consequences for our actions and sins. Yet we have a merciful and loving God who will forgive us our sins. Friend, you and I will make messy decisions. We may turn away from God and follow the teachings of this secular culture, but the Holy Spirit will bring us to repentance, and God will still work through us to bring to completion His will. We can trust that even if we don't recognize it in the moment, God still uses us for His greater work, even if our life is messy and our past is dishonorable.

The Psalms offer guidance:

I waited patiently for the Lord; He inclined to me and heard my cry. He drew me up from the pit of destruction, out of the miry bog, and set my feet upon a rock, making my steps secure. He put a new song in my mouth, a song of praise to our God. Many will see and fear, and put their trust in the Lord. (Psalm 40:1–3)

God will draw us up from our destruction and will make our path secure. He will fill us with praise and allow others to see His work done through us so that they may believe in Him too.

TREASURES IN JARS OF CLAY

These moments of affliction and struggle remind us that God is the ultimate protector and deliverer. We are reminded of this in 2 Corinthians. Paul wrote to the Corinthians to help unite them. They'd had hurt among themselves, and Paul used part of his letter to remind them that God was working through them.

The lesson of treasures in jars of clay in chapter 4 deserves attention for its powerful imagery. Can you picture it? A clay item will break at a drop. Yet that clay jar is temporary. Shattering it reveals the treasure inside:

> **But we have this treasure in jars of clay, to show that the surpassing power belongs to God and not to us. We are afflicted in every way, but not crushed; perplexed, but not driven to despair; persecuted, but not forsaken; struck down, but not destroyed.** (2 Corinthians 4:7–9)

We fix our eyes on the treasure (eternal life with Jesus) and not on the vessel (our body) that is weak and fragile like the clay. When obstacles threaten to break us, tear us down, or defeat us, we might be tempted to believe that is the end. We become filled with despair and desperation. Yet when we trust in God during those moments, we can be a witness to others around us. Think of someone you know who, when confronted with an unbearable situation, became a witness of God's mercy and strength to others. Maybe this person has had a heartbreaking falling out with their child but still trusts in God's goodness. Maybe this person has a baby with a chronic illness and throughout all the doctor appointments and hospital visits can see the blessings from God in that baby's baptismal grace.

It's easy to become engulfed by defeat and despair and to have a lack of zeal for life. But we all know people who have used these feelings to talk of Jesus and His sacrifice for us. They use challenges to talk of God's strength. That strength is the same for our mothers who lost a precious baby in miscarriage, for our grandmothers who lost a father or husband in war, and for our friend who is battling cancer.

> **So we do not lose heart. Though our outer self is wasting away, our inner self is being renewed day by day. For this light momentary affliction is preparing for us an eternal weight of glory beyond all comparison.** (2 Corinthians 4:16–17)

Our outer self will continue to weaken, but our inner self will be with Christ Jesus in heaven one day. Then, on the Last Day, Jesus will raise our bodies and glorify them like His glorious risen body. That is the promise we can rest in.

Paul reminds us that God works through us to share the Gospel with

MYTH 4: GOD WON'T GIVE YOU MORE THAN YOU CAN HANDLE

others around us. He understands that we will suffer, for he suffered too. But with that suffering comes the opportunity to lean even more on Jesus, to share the Gospel and the hope we have because of His work in our lives:

> **We are affiliated in every way, but not crushed; perplexed, but not driven to despair; persecuted, but not forsaken; struck down, but not destroyed; always carrying in the body the death of Jesus, so that the life of Jesus may be manifested in our bodies.** (2 Corinthians 4:8–10)

Our jars of clay will always shatter, but may we remember that the jar is not what's important. It's the treasure inside the jar. It's Jesus. It's eternal life with Him in the new heavens and the new earth where we will never be damaged or met with struggle and affliction. May we rest in that promise.

Let's take a look at 1 Corinthians 10:13: "No temptation has overtaken you that is not common to man. God is faithful, and He will not let you be tempted beyond your ability, but with the temptation He will also provide the way of escape, that you may be able to endure it." People so often use this passage to explain that God will not give us anything we can't handle. Yet that's not what this passage says. This passage speaks about our temptations, not our situations in this life. It's important that we don't take verses out of context. Here, we are given a comfort to remind us to turn to God and to rely on His strength. This is not meant to cover up people's struggles and the pain they are facing. For example, following my cousin's murder, I remained in my faith, and God has comforted me with the reminder that she is with Jesus in heaven.

GOD'S WILL BE DONE EVEN DURING THE PAIN WE FACE

Jesus had feelings of sorrow and despair, just like we do:

> **Then He said to them, "My soul is very sorrowful, even to death; remain here, and watch with Me." And going a little farther He fell on His face and prayed, saying, "My Father, if it be possible, let this cup pass from Me; nevertheless, not as I will, but as You will."** (Matthew 26:38–39)

Jesus felt deep anguish and even asked God, if possible, to take the suffering from Him.

GOD'S ENCOURAGING WORD

Yet God the Son knew what was required of Him. Jesus knew He would be crucified and suffer death on the cross for sins that He didn't commit. Jesus felt the horror of what was to happen to Him and prayed so hard that He fell to His knees and drops of blood formed on His brow.

After praying, Jesus rested His heart. His will is to follow God's will.

Friend, we are going to have moments of abject sorrow. We are going to struggle with things that our minds cannot comprehend: unthinkable traumas and unsolvable problems. Let us learn from Jesus. We can go to God in prayer with all the despair and sorrow and defeat of our lives. We bring our concerns, voice our frustrations, and cry out our grief.

Even as we pour out our feelings, we can rest in the assurance that God already knows what is on our hearts, and He is merciful. He will work everything for our good. His will—our forgiveness and salvation in Jesus—will be done!

PRAYER:

Heavenly Father,
Thank You for walking with me as I navigate hard trials during my life. There are moments that are so often hard to speak about or put into words. Yet You know my heart and provide comfort for me. Forgive me when I rely on my own strength to get me through hard times. Remind me of Your grace and mercy during those situations when it is hard for me to notice them. Lead me to You in prayer to lean on Your strength to get me through times of hurt, frustration, and grief.
In Jesus' name. Amen.

GENTLE REMINDERS:

- God allows things to happen so His strength can be shown through them.

- May we lean on God, not ourselves.

- Pray for peace and to trust in God and His will, not in your own understanding.

MYTH 4: GOD WON'T GIVE YOU MORE THAN YOU CAN HANDLE

JOURNAL PROMPT:

What is hard for you right now or was in the past? When were you made aware of your strength failing and God's strength truly strengthening you?

MYTH 5
FIND YOUR INNER PEACE

"Find your inner peace and heal your soul."

"Peace begins from within."

"Good vibes only."

"We can never obtain peace in the outer world,
until we make peace with ourselves." —Dalai Lama

I wake to the sounds of my youngest crying out to me. Morning has officially started. Now the tasks are getting everyone ready and navigating the sass of a three-year-old wanting to choose her clothes for the day. (She does know we're late, right?) The hustle and bustle of our weekday mornings beg the question, "Does this qualify as an Olympic sport?" If so, we could medal.

Maybe your mornings are not hectic. Maybe it's your nights or afternoons that have a degree of chaos you desperately want to control. Our sinful flesh wants to believe we can do it all on our own. We live in a world that tells us, "Do you lack peace? Is your world chaotic? Buy our product or service and it will all go away!" Then we look at our lives and see the chaos, often blind to the joys woven throughout it. The wild mornings trying to get out the door, the after-school meltdowns when we are the only parent home to navigate all the emotions, the turmoil of family relationships at holiday gatherings, or the deadline for work that snuck up on us on Friday afternoon. Whatever your chaos may be, according to society, there's an app, a workshop, or a book for that.

So we download, attend, and read them all. Give me the one for organizing my closet. Now, I'll never take more than two minutes to pick out my clothes. Give me the meal prep app or service. Now, cooking dinner will never be a problem (even if some of the people at the table require

MYTH 5: FIND YOUR INNER PEACE

me to serve mac and cheese with dino nuggets and a side of yogurt). Give me the flawless morning routine that will leave me refreshed and renewed even though I was up three times in the night. It can substitute for a plain ol' good night's rest, right? Feeling overwhelmed? Make sure your crystal is recharged. Not sure what choice to make on a job offer or whether to get serious with the guy you're dating? Consult a psychic who'll tell you what to do.

Contemporary culture tells us again and again that these apps, crystals, and mantras are meant to help us. These sound like actions we can take to create our own little sliver of peace. Trust me, as someone who advocates for mental health and healthy habits, there is a place for some of these tools. But some of these things are outside our control. What do we do when such things are what's causing the most turmoil in our lives? We can download a horoscope app, but it won't come to our rescue. Psychics can't see beyond what's physically in front of them. When hard decisions or challenges or generic chaos of daily life make us fall to our knees with tears, these things leave us empty. There is only one who can bring us legitimate comfort: Jesus.

NEW AGE: IS THAT JUST FOR NON-CHRISTIANS?

One way of thinking in our society is based on New Age beliefs, such as belief in reincarnation, astrology, psychics, and the presence of spiritual energy in physical objects like mountains or trees. According to Pew Research Center, roughly six in ten American adults accept at least one of these New Age beliefs.[6] Specifically, four in ten believe in psychics and that spiritual energy can be found in physical objects, while somewhat smaller shares express belief in reincarnation (33 percent) and astrology (29 percent). While these stats show that many Americans hold this type of belief, what blew my mind was this next stat.

Eight in ten Christians say they believe in God as described in the Bible, but six in ten believe in one or more of the four New Age beliefs.[7] *Some* believe in God but *also* believe the New Age ideas? That may be why some of these myths that are wrapped in New Age beliefs sound so familiar. We say them because what's the harm, right? The truth is that if we are not going to discipline it, we are tolerating it.

I can't say "Let me check my horoscope" or "Just send me the good vibes today" and act like that is what controls the universe, not God. We can follow the world or we can follow Christ, but we can't do both. We cannot serve two masters. We either serve God or serve this world and its beliefs.

Some people say this isn't that big of a deal. Yet I push back on that thought. Is your eternal life not a big deal? Is your heart and true inner peace not a big deal? Honestly, if something is not leading me to Christ, why would I want to entertain it? Why would I chance having something lead me astray instead of rooting me more firmly in God's Word? Engaging in practices like reading horoscopes, consulting psychics, and believing in reincarnation or spiritual energy in physical objects is a dangerous game to play, and I'd rather guard my heart than tempt it.

FALSE TEACHING IS ALL AROUND US

Maybe you've been around people who practice using crystals, reading palms, consulting tarot cards, or channeling their psychic vision. Or maybe you haven't, and it's something you have only seen on television or social media. My experience is firsthand.

If you know my family, then you know we love to get together. I'm incredibly blessed that my aunts, uncles, cousins, and grandparents are the people I hung out with almost weekly growing up. The majority of us all lived in the same small town, so that helps, but we truly do love hanging out with one another. My parent's house is the hub of a lot of our get-togethers. Football game? Yep! Random Friday night? Sure! Birthdays, holidays, anniversaries? Of course! This is something I've grown to love. Our home truly was filled with laughter and love.

At one of our get-togethers, I had come home from college for the weekend and was excited to see everyone. In our small town, neighbors as well as relatives would come over to watch games or just chat. Toward the end of that night, as the crowd was dispersing, only a few neighbors and my immediate family members were left. We were outside in the garage when a neighbor came up to me and asked if she could read my palm.

MYTH 5: FIND YOUR INNER PEACE

Spoiler alert: I'm a people pleaser. I'm currently working on it, but nineteen-year-old Faith was in full pleasing mode. Maybe you can relate.

She asked to read my palm, and before I could grasp what was happening, she grabbed my hand and started to "read" it. Friend, this is where guarding our hearts matters. To the outside world, it can look harmless. We might think, *So what, she's looking at lines on your hand and telling you you'll have macaroni art in your fridge one day. She believes in it, even if I don't, so it's no big deal.* In that moment, as I stood on those red steps leading to the garage, I could either accept that she "had the gift," or I could remind myself that God's plan for me will be revealed in His timing, and, as it's revealed, I can trust in His provision and His calling. It's to Him that I turn when I am feeling anxious about the future, not a palm reader.

GUARDING OUR HEARTS

What does God say about guarding our hearts? Protecting our hearts is a theme that comes up so many times in the Bible. We can turn to the wisdom of Proverbs 4:23: "Keep your heart with all vigilance, for from it flow the springs of life." The expression "from it flow the springs of life" suggests that what is in our heart flows outward, including to the people around us. Luke 6:45 teaches us that the heart can be either good or evil. If everything flows from our hearts, then what do we need to allow in, and what should we keep out? An analogy someone once told me is this: "Everyone is given a keyboard. This keyboard inputs into your brain and your heart. The people you interact with and allow to speak into you hold that keyboard. Treat it accordingly." This still sticks with me. The crowd I hang out with matters, what I listen to matters, and the books I read and the shows I watch matter. These are seemingly small things, but they have a mighty impact.

Since we know that a heart is tender and from it flows the springs of life, let's look at the vigilance needed to protect it. *Vigilance*, or *vigilant*, means "the action or state of keeping careful watch for possible danger or difficulties." Friend, we live in a sinful world. There is danger all around, and we can use God's Word and ask the Holy Spirit to protect

GOD'S ENCOURAGING WORD

us, or we can shrug our shoulders and say, "Well, it's not like someone got hurt." (Of course, just because sin didn't hurt someone physically doesn't mean they aren't hurt emotionally or mentally.)

As believers in Christ Jesus, we know that sin will happen in this fallen world. We look to the hope found in Jesus' resurrection and the promise of eternal life with God in heaven. However, what if you don't believe in that promise and believe instead in the crystal on your desk or the cards laid out by your bed? One provides you with comfort and a promise, while the other puts the blame and hardship on you. Would you really have had a better day if only you had charged that crystal or burned that incense or heeded your horoscope? New Age practices are a broken and empty promise.

We, as Christians, have something empty too: an empty tomb, and with it, the resurrection of Jesus Christ and the promise of eternity with Him.

LET'S LOOK TO GOD'S WORD

God's Word is filled with so many things that can help us. An example is this prayer for spiritual strength:

> For this reason I bow my knees before the Father, from whom every family in heaven and on earth is named, that according to the riches of His glory He may grant you to be strengthened with power through His Spirit in your inner being, so that Christ may dwell in your hearts through faith—that you, being rooted and grounded in love, may have strength to comprehend with all the saints what is the breadth and length and height and depth, and to know the love of Christ that surpasses knowledge, that you may be filled with all the fullness of God. Now to Him who is able to do far more abundantly than all that we ask or think, according to the power at work within us, to Him be glory in the church and in Christ Jesus throughout all generations, forever and ever. Amen. (Ephesians 3:14–21)

God gives us prayers and lessons throughout the Bible for us to learn from and remember when we need encouragement and comfort and when we are praising God. The Scriptures are given for our daily use and to inform every aspect of our lives.

MYTH 5: FIND YOUR INNER PEACE

FALSE TEACHERS

We gain insight from Paul in 1 Timothy when he went to minister to the Ephesians. Paul was providing encouragement to Timothy, a young pastor:

> **If anyone teaches a different doctrine and does not agree with the sound words of our Lord Jesus Christ and the teaching that accords with godliness, he is puffed up with conceit and understands nothing.** (1 Timothy 6:3-4)

Timothy was dealing with false teachers just like we do. Modern-day society is filled with false teachers, from the "anything goes" churches down the road from us to the social media accounts we visit. The result of this is shown in the statistics given earlier: a great number of Christians believe in false teachings. When we look for peace and understanding from things other than Jesus and God's Word, we are following a false teaching.

In 1 John 2:23, John reminds us that "no one who denies the Son has the Father. Whoever confesses the Son has the Father also." We confess and believe that Jesus lived a sinless life, died and was crucified, rose again on the third day, and now sits at the right hand of God in heaven. This is what we believe and what we put our faith in. This world has nothing to offer that comes close to that.

SPIRIT OF THE WORLD OR OF THE ONE FROM GOD?

We can turn to Paul's words to the church in Corinth, a community wrecked by division. The people there were living in excess and behaving according to the flesh, not to God's Word. Paul wrote to them to help unite them. Corinth reminds me of today's society. We are also wrecked by division and find ourselves talking more about our divisions than our similarities. Don't believe me? Go turn on your television and watch that twenty-four-hour news cycle. My advice: Turn off your television and go hang out with your loved ones. You'll have more impact on society doing that than you will watching the latest headline crawl across your screen.

Back to Paul and the Corinthians. Paul spoke about divisions and excesses such as sexual immorality, the local congregation, and lawsuits. What I want to draw our attention to is how the Corinthians believed their wisdom was better than God's. Paul took them to task:

> **Let no one deceive himself. If anyone among you thinks that he is wise in this age, let him become a fool that he may become wise.** (1 Corinthians 3:18)

According to this world and human understanding, God's wisdom is foolish. Christians may be ridiculed and persecuted because we believe that a perfect man walked this earth, died on the cross, and rose again to give us eternal life in heaven. We may get told we are crazy to believe that Jonah could live for three days in the belly of a fish, that the ark could hold so many animals, and that the world was created in six days. Somehow, some people find it easier to believe that millions of years ago, a mysterious tiny dot in the universe turned into all of what we see in nature and through telescopes. Personally, I don't think evolution is believable or fulfilling and comforting. But the creation account in the Bible is all that and more.

The same can be said for New Age beliefs. We are told that you need levels of awareness or a great spiritual awakening to have wisdom. When we want to learn more, we search the internet, consult the scientific community, or meet with a psychic in an attempt to gain our peace or help us make decisions. We are constantly bombarded with conversations about turning to this person or that object.

So, how do we become spiritual or of the Spirit? We want to make sure we are of the Spirit of God, not the spirit of this world. The spirit of this world is Satan, and he will do everything he can to influence our decisions for the short term and draw our attention away from the Lord. The Spirit of God does the opposite; the Holy Spirit gives us faith in the life to come, sustains that faith through the means of grace (the Word of God and the sacraments of Baptism and Holy Communion), and points us toward God. This is what we truly need as we navigate our short time here on this earth.

The Spirit of God comes to us through God's Word and the gift of

MYTH 5: FIND YOUR INNER PEACE

Holy Baptism. Through the water and the Word, God gives us a gift that imparts "a secret and hidden wisdom of God, which God decreed before the ages for our glory" (1 Corinthians 2:7).

We are reminded in Matthew 18:3–4,

Truly, I say to you, unless you turn and become like children, you will never enter the kingdom of heaven. Whoever humbles himself like this child is the greatest in the kingdom of heaven.

PEACE OF GOD SURPASSES UNDERSTANDING

The apostle Paul knew well that there were many things outside his control, yet by faith in Jesus, he possessed an incredible peace despite spending half of his ministry in prison—not exactly the ideal circumstances for a missionary. In Philippians 4, wrapping up his letter to the church in Philippi, he reminds the church to not be anxious. Philippians 4:4–13 is one of the better-known passages of the Bible. Here are two passages that apply to our discussion in this chapter:

Do not be anxious about anything. (Philippians 4:5)

I can do all things through Christ who strengthens me. (Philippians 4:13)

These verses are wonderful encouragement to us, but I want to look more closely at a different part of this passage:

And the peace of God, which surpasses all understanding, will guard your hearts and your minds in Christ Jesus. (Philippians 4:7)

The "peace of God" surpasses *all* understanding. In our constant busyness and chronic frustration and absence of feeling like we're in control, this peace seems like foolishness. And it still seems foolish when we understand that Paul was jailed for his ministry work during an era when people didn't survive jail. Jesus called Paul to teach and preach, to witness and heal. But he wasn't free to do that work, so how could there be a peace about him?

Paul explains that this peace comes from God.

What does it mean to surpass our understanding? The definition of *surpass* is "to be greater than." In this context, God's peace is greater than our understanding. This side of heaven, we will never understand it. (That doesn't stop us from trying, does it?)

We may see this peace with our loved ones who are facing death or dealing with a chronic illness. We see them struggling day in and day out, overwhelmed and exhausted, yet they have a peace about them that is hard to comprehend. We question, "How can you be at peace? You've prayed for healing, but you're still sick."

I'm reminded of my grandpa Smokey as he laid in a hospital bed. Lung cancer had begun to completely overtake him. His lung capacity was so low that I could see him labor for each breath he took. Yet there was a peace about him. Our entire family crowded that room, each of us taking a moment to say our goodbyes. We cried, and he shed a few tears, but he still found ways to crack jokes. People may wonder how can you joke when you're so close to death. It surpasses all understanding, doesn't it?

It's because Smokey knew that his last physical breath wasn't the end. He knew that Jesus was waiting with arms wide open, waiting to welcome him, to rejoice with him, and take away every pain and ache afflicting him here on earth. We can have peace at the end of this life because we are confident in the eternal life Jesus won for us on the cross:

> **Jesus said to her, "I am the resurrection and the life. Whoever believes in Me, though he die, yet shall he live, and everyone who lives and believes in Me shall never die."** (John 11:25-26)

Did we feel sadness, grief, and maybe even some anger that Smokey left us before we wanted him to? Yes. But we can have those emotions and still have the peace that can only come from God. Again, this surpasses all understanding. This peace is not an emotion within us but is a gift of the Holy Spirit that comes from outside us.

The world tells us this isn't so. If we believe that our circumstances are a result of how God thinks about us, we will be disappointed, fearful, and anxious about our relationship with Him. This type of thinking is rooted in selfishness. It leads us down the road of placing our confidence in

MYTH 5: FIND YOUR INNER PEACE

ourselves, not in Christ. We look to what we want, not what God wants for us or for His will to be done. But is it even possible to do God's will?

We see a perfect example of submitting to God's will when Jesus prayed in the Garden of Gethsemane in Matthew 26:39: "My Father, if it be possible, let this cup pass from Me; nevertheless, not as I will, but as You will." Jesus obediently leaned into God's will, even though it meant pain and death. Jesus put His trust in God's will (for Him and for the whole world), not the overwhelming feelings He was experiencing as a true man.

With faith that the Holy Spirit imparts to us, we can look to our heavenly Father as the source of our strength. Just as the serpent tempted Eve to be independent of God, this world tells us to be independent. Yet as Christians, we are dependent on Jesus.

Jesus is what makes us spiritual. All of the world's "spirituality" is no replacement for Jesus. But the secular world tells us that we make our own peace. This is impossible. We are sinful. The kind of peace we seek is not just an absence of busyness or arguing at the dinner table or hitting only green lights on our morning commute. This kind of peace doesn't come from holding a rock in our hands or someone else looking down into our palm and looking at the lines there. This peace is not internal. It's the fruit of the Spirit:

But the fruit of the Spirit is love, joy, peace, patience, kindness, goodness, faithfulness, gentleness, self-control; against such things there is no law. (Galatians 5:22–23)

This comes to us with no limits. It comes from the Lord of peace Himself. And He gives us this peace when and how we need it—which is all the time:

Now may the Lord of peace Himself give you peace at all times in every way. The Lord be with you all. (2 Thessalonians 3:16)

How did it happen that this peace we can receive at all times and in all ways came to us in the first place? Because God sent His Son to suffer and die for the sins of the world. How does it come into your life and mine? Because of Baptism. One of the blessings of Baptism is faith in

Jesus' work on the cross, in His death to atone for our sins, and in His resurrection from the grave that proves His power to defeat death. Now we have His peace that so many are searching for.

So many people in this world are struggling without this peace. Yet they yearn for it, so they are doing all they can to fill the void. That's why horoscopes, tarot cards, crystals, and psychics are so prevalent. And these industries keep growing because the more people fail, the more they look to these industries to give them peace. Such things impose a very real danger because they do not come from our Prince of Peace. Rather, they come from a place of harm and destruction that calls us away from Christ and His grace.

JESUS IS NOT A FEELING

New Age practices will tell us that spirituality is all in what we do and *feel*. You'll often hear the question "Do you feel the energy?" People will talk about your aura and how you need to cleanse it or about aligning your chakras.

Paul reminds us in 1 Corinthians 3:18,

Let no one deceive himself. If anyone among you thinks that he is wise in this age, let him become a fool so that he may become wise.

There is nothing wrong with social media in itself, nothing wrong with print media in itself. All of it can be used to help spread the Gospel—or to try to hide or distort it. The godless voices of the world say it's smart to turn to social media or broadcast media for wisdom and guidance for living our lives, but just like true peace, such sources do not give us true wisdom. True wisdom is in God's Word. Wisdom is learning to let go of our self-focused desires to be in control (and being the masters of our own lives) in order to humble ourselves, admit our flaws, confess our sins, and repent of them, laying our issues, burdens, and joys at the foot of the cross. True wisdom is spending more time studying God's Word, more time hearing the Gospel proclaimed in church, more time in prayerful conversation with God than we do scrolling our feeds. This takes humility. Admitting that we might not be the smartest person

MYTH 5: FIND YOUR INNER PEACE

in the room isn't easy. In fact, it's so hard that most of us don't truly get there.

Chapter 2 addressed making ourselves into idols. (I once saw it defined like this: Edging God Out: E.G.O.) It's important for us to learn to separate our feelings from our identity. But, as we've been discussing, this is countercultural. The world tells us "I feel (insert emotion), therefore I am (insert emotion)." This is a step toward making our feelings our idol. It is the ultimate flesh talking and often leads to destruction.

For example, in the middle of my fourth trimester with my first child, I was diagnosed with postpartum depression. (Reminder: If you or someone you know is struggling after having a baby, don't brush it off with, "Oh, she's just tired." *Please* speak with your ob-gyn, nurse practitioner, husband, mother, sister, pastor, or therapist. It's important to be proactive about those thoughts instead of suppressing or hiding them. Even if the thoughts seem minor or typical, it is important to *talk to someone*.) During that time, I often didn't feel like I loved my child. I felt like I had lost a part of myself, and I became depressed. I could have let that feeling overwhelm and overtake me. Instead, I sought and found assistance from people God worked through to help me. I didn't "feel" God, but He was still there supporting, healing, and loving me.

Our feelings were created by God to help us navigate relationships in this world. They are meant to protect us and guide us as we go through trials and joys on this side of heaven. But sin has distorted our feelings and emotions just as it has our thoughts and desires. We need to be careful not to let feelings become our identity.

Our society says exactly the opposite. When people express a feeling, either we can accept that feeling as fact, or we can help diffuse the emotion and remind them of the facts of Christ's compassion for us. Often, though, people may be afraid to be "canceled" and say instead, "Yes, your feelings are what God says about you." It's a sad reality that many churches in America today promote fleeting feelings as lasting truth and evidence of God's will. This is why knowing the Word of God and holding our congregation and church leaders to it is so important.

GOD'S ENCOURAGING WORD

Friend, Jesus is more than a feeling. If we equate Jesus to a feeling, then when we are feeling lost and struggling, we might believe that Jesus is as fickle as our emotions, that if we don't *feel* Him, then He is not with us. This can cause us to put our faith and trust into something tangible. For example, during the trauma of postpartum depression, I didn't feel Jesus there. I felt forgotten, just like David. Yet like David, with the power of the Holy Spirit, I didn't stay in that feeling and make it my identity. Christian professionals, friends, and family members came alongside me as I worked through the turmoil. I say with confidence that my hope is in God.

> Hope in God; for I shall again praise Him, my salvation and my God. (Psalm 42:11)

PRAYER:

Heavenly Father,
Thank You for giving us hope in Christ Jesus. Thank You for being the peace we can rest and take comfort in even when we don't understand that peace. Forgive us for going to worldly things and false teachers to find comfort. Forgive us for equating Your Son, Jesus, with what we feel in a particular moment. Help us to lean on Your will and not our own understanding. May the Holy Spirit do a good work in us and bring us peace.
In Jesus' name. Amen.

GENTLE REMINDERS:

- Look to God's Word, not to false teachers.
- The Holy Spirit, not the world, is working in us.
- Jesus is not a feeling.
- We have a peace that passes all understanding.

MYTH 5: FIND YOUR INNER PEACE

JOURNAL PROMPT:

Do you equate Jesus to a feeling? What "spiritual" practices have you incorporated in your life that you thought were harmless but could be leading you away from God?

MYTH 6
PRAY HARDER

"I worked so hard, and my dream didn't happen."

"My prayer didn't get answered."

"Keep praying, and God will give you what you want."

"I guess I didn't pray for the right thing."

I've just sent my kids off to daycare and my husband off to work. It's summer in our house, so our schedule is a little wild. My husband, an assistant principal, does administrative things during the summer. And I'm working on this book, along with working toward a master's degree in trauma and resilience, so this mama welcomes the help that daycare can provide.

I make myself a cup of hot coffee and ignore the dishes that are piled high. (We are spending more time at the neighborhood splash pad eating PB&Js than in our kitchen.) There is a lack of clean mugs, so I reach into the back of the cupboard for a mug for my delicious, hot (not lukewarm) coffee. (Mom win!)

The mug I pull out makes me smile. I'm a little obsessed with coffee mugs. Funny saying? Yes! Bible verse? Absolutely! A phrase like "Mama Bear" or "Hello Beautiful"? Of course!

I found today's mug by scrolling online. (Yes, your typical millennial just scrolling social media, finding the cutest mug, and clicking buy.) The mug has an image of a campfire on the front, and while I don't camp, I love the mug because of the saying on it: "God is greater than the highs and lows." On the back side are the symbols for that phrase: G>^v. At one time, this mug was in perfect condition, a crisp blue color with the bold decals. Now, not so much. The only symbol that is still totally intact is the G, while the rest fades with each wash.

MYTH 6: PRAY HARDER

There was a season when I drank from this mug daily. It was my go-to mug for coffee in the morning and tea at night. Throughout this life, we all have different seasons. In our family, we call them high or low seasons. High seasons are filled with the laughter, joy, and happiness of a job promotion, the birth of a baby, a note from a special friend. Low seasons are when sadness, grief, and depression are at the center of our attention because of the death of a loved one or because you or a family member got laid off. High and low seasons ebb and flow and are often mixed together. Sometimes, I don't realize I'm in a high season until I've hit my low and recognize what's missing. Other times, I don't realize I'm in a low season until someone points it out or until things have started to look up. In any case, we want to live according to God's will.

THE PRESSURE ON OUR CHILDREN

It won't always be raining, but it won't always be blooming either. The world wants us to believe that every moment of our lives needs to be blooming. "If you're not growing, you're dying." "Think it, achieve it, seize it." Recent data indicates that the proportion of people experiencing anxiety and depression is at an all-time high. According to a 2023 Gallup study, 29 percent of adults in the United States have depression, which is ten points higher than in 2015.[8]

When I'm not writing or cohosting a podcast or teaching the coolest six-year-olds, I'm working on my graduate studies. I spend a lot of time with research materials, particularly about the effects that our society and its way of living have on children and adults, and with textbooks about social and emotional health.

That puts me in the middle of a storm that pertains to children and their mental health. Truthfully, this topic has become my soapbox. I'll talk about it at length and with anyone: the pressure we are putting on our children, the scheduling we are forcing on them and on ourselves, and so on.

A few years ago, someone asked me, "Where's the white space in your calendar?" Confused, I asked, "White space? What are you talking about?" The person replied, "If I were to look at your calendar, where is there just white space where nothing is scheduled so it's blank?"

Did that give you a gut punch? I was completely taken aback by that question. This was asked of me during a busy season while I had a newborn and my husband was working on his master's degree. "White space? You mean the time I'm sleeping?" Since that time, my family and I have been incredibly intentional about our white space. We have "nothing" weekends, we plan downtime by scheduling nothing. This helps us take time to just relax and enjoy one another.

Our world tells parents that for their children to be successful, the kids need to participate in everything. Every sport. Every club. Every school event. Now, before I go on my full soapbox rant, here is a disclaimer. Sports, theater, music, scouts, camp, and similar activities outside of school aren't bad things. Rather, there are many benefits to activities like these, such as learning responsibility and teamwork, honing a skill, nurturing a talent, and creating lasting friendships. But the problem begins when these activities become the end-all-be-all of the family's life.

"Sorry, we didn't make it to church; we had a baseball game." When does wanting to help children learn and participate in extracurriculars become more important than time with Jesus? This is a slippery slope. Next thing we know, we're telling ourselves, "Well, if they want a chance at playing college ball, they *have* to do this." "Everyone else is, so they need to do it too." "This is how she earns scholarships for college."

When deciding whether to participate in activities like these, we have to ask about the end goal. Is it that your child becomes a Division I athlete? Is it for him to create friendships? Is it for her to be awarded scholarship money? All of those are great goals, but what is the sacrifice to the family? Research from the Gallup study shows that more than 15 percent of teens had a major depressive episode last year.[9] Some studies indicate that when children are pushed hard, they are left burned out and defeated by the time they are teenagers.[10]

In the thick of parenting, we want what is best for our child. I totally understand that. My daughter is not even five, and my husband and I

MYTH 6: PRAY HARDER

have already had multiple conversations about these things. To the outside world, we look crazy. Why wouldn't we put her in dance during the school year? It's only once a week. Other parents may feel pressed to hire private coaches for their son in baseball or hire a talent coach and an agent so she can model or enter pageants.

Our family opts out of these things so we can have downtime. We want the white space. We trust Jesus will provide a productive and fruitful life for her without constant obligations.

That said, we acknowledge that as long as activities are kept in a healthy balance with time to rest and regenerate, they can be beneficial for learning social skills, for staying physically active, and for nurturing creativity. Parents benefit, too, when friendships develop.

The big lie about extracurriculars is that more is better and that winning is everything. We start to feel like we're bad parents if our kids don't have a calendar full of learning experiences, playdates, or year-round sports. Parents want their kids to be happy, and if happy means they participate in everything available so they don't feel left out, then that's what we do for them. We give in to pressure to provide the best life for our kids, and in turn, we pressure our kids to keep busy all the time and not take time to just be.

Pushing kids to achieve and succeed, to work hard and win, might cause actual emotional and physical harm. Young kids may suffer lasting injury when pushed beyond their limits in sports and activities like gymnastics and dance. Young minds can be troubled if the child doesn't make the big league and get the professional sports contract.

Adults do the same thing to themselves. We're told to work hard and play hard. The harder we work, the more money we'll make and the happier we'll be. To be clear: More money will not bring you more happiness. Statistically, it's proven that happiness peaks at an income of around $100,000 annually;[11] happiness plateaus within half of one percent above or below that amount. In other words, people who make $200,000 are not markedly happier than people who make $100,00. That doesn't stop people from striving for more money though.

SERVING GOD AND RESTING

According to the 2024 World Happiness Report, for the last seven years, Finland has been named the happiest country in the world. There is a calm and easy-going lifestyle and an attitude that less is okay in Finland. Not so much in the United States, where the American dream is defined by wealth, power, busyness, work, and stuff.

It won't surprise you that the contemporary American definition of happiness, realizing that dream of success, is not supported in Scripture. God gives all of us incredible vocations. This may be the vocation of being a parent and raising your children at home. It could be the vocation of writing, teaching, or using your gifts such as singing or fostering relationships to serve God. God gives us vocations that suit our seasons of life: being a child, a spouse, a parent, a grandparent. He also gives us skills specific to providing for ourselves and our families by working at a job outside the home.

Working to the best of your ability and using the skills and talents God has gifted you with is admirable and God-pleasing, but it doesn't mean we abandon our need for rest. God Himself gave us this structure when He created the world in six days and rested on the seventh.

Ecclesiastes 3:1 says,

For everything there is a season, and a time for every matter under heaven.

God created the seasons of the year and the seasons of our life. If we continue in chapter 3, King Solomon identified different times in our lives: "a time to break down, and a time to build up" (v. 3) and "a time to keep silence, and time to speak" (v. 7).

In today's world, we are tempted to think of rest as physical: the kind of rest equated to eight hours of sleep at night. Yet there are different types of rest, including physical, emotional, mental, and spiritual. Let's take a look at each.

Physical rest correlates to our bodies. This can include our sleep habits and the use of our muscles. Research shows that kids are tearing

MYTH 6: PRAY HARDER

ligaments sooner and more often due to a lack of rest and overuse.[12] When we take time to rest either by getting truly adequate sleep or just enjoying the sun while sitting on the patio, we are providing rest for our bodies.

Emotional rest was unfamiliar to me until I attended therapy for my trauma. We had just finished a session that I had cried throughout when my therapist said, "Now, you need to rest for the next twenty-four hours." Still sobbing, I asked, "Why do I need to rest? All I did was cry." My therapist explained that emotional exhaustion may occur during unrest. According to the Mayo Clinic, emotional exhaustion is when stress accumulates from continuous negative or challenging events and you are in a state of feeling emotionally drained.[13] We can help relieve this exhaustion by releasing pent-up tension and emotions through crying, talking, movement (such as walking), or journaling. Rest is key to letting us honor our feelings and process them in a healthy way.

Mental health is helped when we rest our brains by taking breaks. Our brains can only gather and retain so much information at a time. Anything beyond this capacity is called cognitive overload. That's when our brains stop absorbing information and sensation and gloss over stimuli. Instead, a practice called interlacing is beneficial. Interlacing is when periods of learning are interrupted by some other type of activity. For example, at schools in Finland, for every forty-five-minute period of learning, there is a fifteen-minute period of play.[14] Studies show that incorporating movement in learning will help the brain retain information longer and store it in long-term memory instead of just short-term.[15]

The last and most important is spiritual rest. Many of us need a reminder that our Creator established rest for us and designed us for rest. Specifically, by God's model, we are to set aside the regular routine of work and take time to worship with our brothers and sisters in Christ, hear the Gospel, receive the Lord's Supper, and enjoy the fruits of our labor:

> Remember the Sabbath day, to keep it holy. Six days you shall labor, and do all your work, but the seventh day is a Sabbath to the Lord your God. On it you shall not do any work, you, or your son, or your

daughter, your male servant, or your female servant, or your livestock, or the sojourner who is within your gates. For in six days the Lord made heaven and earth, the sea, and all that is in them, and rested on the seventh day. Therefore the Lord blessed the Sabbath day and made it holy. (Exodus 20:8–11)

The New Testament gives us several examples of Jesus resting. In Mark, after traveling to teach and minister, after sending out the apostles to teach and minister, and still with much to do, Jesus told His apostles to take a break: "Come away by yourselves to a desolate place and rest a while" (6:31). And in Luke 5:16, Jesus took time to go away and to pray. In Matthew 14:22–23, He spent the evening alone, praying. In Luke 22:41, He "withdrew . . . knelt down and prayed."

There are other examples of times when Jesus separated Himself from people and work to rest and to pray. God put these examples in the Bible to remind us that even Jesus rested. We live in a world that tells us to keep going and work hard. Sunday is no longer the Lord's day; it's the day to get the laundry done, the car washed, and cart your children to whatever activities they are enrolled in. These things need to be done. But I pray that we can prioritize God as the First Commandment reminds us and balance our lives so we take time to rest and to worship our Creator and Lord.

PLANTING SEEDS

As shown above, we live in a world that focuses on extrinsic value, not on God's will for us. In childhood, this revolves around sports and activities, but adulthood looks a little different. Grown-ups are asked, "How much money do you bring to the table?" "What do you do for a living?" "What car do you drive?" "How big is your house?" "What neighborhood do you live in?" "How much are you saving for retirement or college or vacation?"

These questions feed our dreams for our lives. Sometimes these dreams reflect our sinful human nature. Sometimes our goals and ambitions are healthy and productive and align with a God-pleasing life. But what if we believe our expectations are aligned with God's will but our dream isn't realized?

MYTH 6: PRAY HARDER

To illustrate this, let's take a look at gardening. We buy seeds, plant them in nutritious soil, water them daily, and sometimes those seeds sprout. But sometimes they won't. Sometimes you're overwhelmed and have tomatoes pouring out of your ears while your cucumbers are small and lacking. The same is true for our dreams. This reminds me of something my husband once said to me. We were praying for something, and I kept saying, "Keep praying. Ask and receive, right?" To which he responded, "Yes, and . . . just because I'm asking doesn't mean God has to say yes."

WILL EVERY PRAYER GET ANSWERED?

Why is it that faithful Christians don't get everything we pray for? Isn't that how this Christianity thing is supposed to work? We pray, and God says, "Yep! Done!"?

Looking back, I'm so thankful God said no or not yet to me. Friend, think back to when you were young; maybe there was a particular person you wanted to date, but now you're saying, "That person wasn't right for me after all." That could be the same with a job that you wanted at the time, but now you're thankful that you weren't hired.

For me, I think of our house. More than a year ago, we were planning to move, and I thought for sure that a certain house was the answer to our prayers. I kept praying, "God, please allow us to get this house." The housing marking was wild, and houses were going off the market before they were even really placed on it. One Sunday, we got the call that our offer on this certain house was accepted. We got the house! We rejoiced and were so thankful. But at two in the morning, my husband woke up and said, "We can't buy that house."

I was shocked. "What? We prayed for this, and we got it." There were a few issues with the house that in the hustle of the offer and acceptance we hadn't paid attention to. In the hours after our offer was accepted though, my husband realized that buying it wasn't a good idea. Our real estate agent wasn't happy to get that phone call. Not long after that, we bought a house through a family friend that was a better fit for us.

GOD'S ENCOURAGING WORD

If we had continued with the purchase of that first house, we would have had to deal with the issues that were problematic and would not be in our current home that better suits our family. I kept praying throughout the whole process: "God, whatever house we get, let it be obvious that the only way we received it was because of You."

As we sat in our new home, I was overwhelmed with tears because our home-buying journey answered that prayer. It was blatantly obvious, not just to fellow believers but others who didn't believe, that we had "luck" on our side. It was made clear through having my dad overhear a conversation about the house being put up for sale, from the buying process being simple and without a hiccup, and with the house fitting our families along with being close to our workplaces. You and I know that it wasn't "luck" but God working things together for our good.

Look to Paul's letter to the Romans as we navigate this topic. Paul wrote, "For God is my witness, whom I serve with my spirit in the gospel of His Son, that without ceasing I mention you always in my prayers, *asking that somehow by God's will I may now at last succeed in coming to you*" (Romans 1:9–10, emphasis added). Paul wanted to be in person to minister to them and share the Gospel. God did not allow that. "I have often intended to come to you (but thus far have been prevented)" (Romans 1:13). Because Paul was prevented from going, the Holy Spirit inspired him to write the letter instead.

Maybe you're like me and wonder, *Wouldn't it have been better for him to be in person? Why didn't God just let him do that?* We will never know. What we do know is the letter that taught the church in Rome about the kingdom of God through the work of Christ Jesus exists so that we can learn from it.

WHEN YOU FALL SHORT OF YOUR DREAM

One day when my husband came home from work, he said, "Faith, you are going to be a Boston Celtics fan." As someone who watches sports only so she can have shoulder-to-shoulder time with her husband, I found his statement hilarious. I laughed and said, "Oh, yeah? Why's that?"

MYTH 6: PRAY HARDER

He said, "You have to hear what the head coach, Joe Mazzulla, said in an interview at the Eastern Conference Finals."

Now, for those not familiar with the NBA, if you win the Eastern Conference Finals, you will head to the Finals, which is the pinnacle series of your entire NBA career. It's where everyone wants to be at the end of the season. It's the thing that little boys dream about and say, "One day . . ." Every NBA player and staff member is working as hard as he or she can to get to that series.

Intrigued, I asked him to clarify, and this is what made me a Joe Mazzulla fan.[16] During the interview, Mazzulla was asked about the Celtics' win-or-die mentality in the context of his coaching career and what he's doing with that personally to not let that consume him. Mazzulla described meeting three terminally ill girls, each under age 21, and seeing that they had a joy for life despite their circumstances. He said, "You always hear people saying thank You and giving glory to God when they are holding a trophy, but you never really hear it in times like this. So for me, it's a time to just sit and just be thankful and faithful. That's what it's about."

You're a fan now, too, aren't you? We can be quick to praise God when our prayers are answered. We give glory when we get the promotion, our kid makes the school play, or a relationship is restored. Praising our heavenly Father is a glorious thing, and we need to do it more. Psalm 9:1 tells us, "I will give thanks to the LORD with my whole heart; I will recount all of Your wonderful deeds." He provides so much for us. So much that we might not even think about it. But when things don't go our way or our prayers aren't answered the way we want, how do we handle *that*?

We can look to David in Psalm 13:1–2:

> How long O LORD? Will You forget me forever? How long will You hide Your face from me? How long must I take counsel in my soul and have sorrow in my heart all the day? How long shall my enemy be exalted over me?

David was being pursued by King Saul, who wanted to kill him. He felt that God had forgotten him and didn't care about his suffering. David wanted to know how long he would have to deal with the situation.

We all have had times when we felt exactly like that. "How long?" "Why is this happening?" "Are You even *listening*, God?"

Sometimes, the answer to the "Why are bad things happening?" question is that we created the circumstances ourselves. "You jumped off the barn roof, and you broke your leg." We are not invincible, and behaviors have consequences. But not every situation has an explanation. Things happen that we can't fathom. In the small traumas and big disasters of our lives exists a tension and mystery that we may never fully understand. We can still trust that God is working for good, that good may be seen on this side of heaven, or maybe it won't. Nevertheless, we can trust that God's ultimate good for us is eternal life with Jesus.

This is all true, but what do we *do* when we or our loved ones are struggling with this question? How do we comfort and support them, help them draw closer to Jesus? I want to preface this next section with a disclaimer about spiritual maturity. Peter tells us in 1 Peter 2:2, "Like newborn infants, long for the pure spiritual milk, that by it you may grow up into salvation." Some of these topics are for newborn infants, and some are for those further in their faith walk. To be most helpful, take inventory of who you are speaking with before you dive into sensitive conversation, and rely on the Holy Spirit to give you words. Going to your pastor for pastoral care can be a great way to help make sure you are ministering to others in a healthy way.

WHY DO BAD THINGS HAPPEN TO GOOD PEOPLE?

We all have prayers that I would call small-scale, even though they feel big in the moment—buying a house, taking that big vacation, or switching jobs. But what about the gut-wrenching prayers? These include prayers when we are curled on the floor, crying, asking, "Why, Lord?" We all go through this. We have a concern on our hearts that hurts so much that we can't even say it out loud. It's a scary thing, a tragedy, a deep wound. With all the technology and treatments and help available to us today, why do bad things continue to happen? And why do they happen to people who don't deserve it?

MYTH 6: PRAY HARDER

The teacher in me is looking for the one-word answer: sin. It corrupts every aspect of God's creation. We first see sin in Genesis 3 during the fall. Our first parents saw it too:

Then the eyes of both were opened and they knew that they were naked. And they sewed fig leaves together and made themselves loincloths. (v. 7)

As we continue to read in Genesis 3, God tells us that sin is here to stay:

I will put enmity between you and the woman, and between your offspring and her offspring. (v. 15)

I will surely multiply your pain in childbearing. (v. 16)

By the sweat of your face you shall eat bread, till you return to the ground" (v. 19)

God's creation was compromised, yet even then God cared for His people: "And the LORD God made for Adam and for his wife garments of skins and clothed them" (v. 21). What comfort for us! Even when our flesh leads us away from God, God still cares for us and provides for us. Goodness will always come from God. Matthew 5:45 states that God indiscriminately pours out goodness for all: "For He makes His sun rise on the evil and on the good, and sends rain on the just and on the unjust."

The simple answer to why bad things happens is sin, but our adult minds struggle with that. A terminal illness, abuse, crime, an emotional trauma, or a debilitating accident happen because sin is everywhere. True, but saying those words doesn't always validate and honor the person who is suffering. I know in my heart this is true, but that knowledge didn't ease the ache and sorrow I felt in the midst of my own trauma.

The biblical account of how God responded to Hannah can help sooth our hearts. Hannah was one of the wives of Elkanah. She had struggled to have a child, while Peninnah, Elkanah's other wife, had children. Every year, Elkanah went up to the mountain to worship and sacrifice (see 1 Samuel 1:3). After the ritual, he would bring back portions of the roasted meat and give a double portion to Hannah because he loved her (see v. 5). In this verse, we see a husband and wife struggling with their prayer not being answered. Hannah not being able to get pregnant was because "the LORD had closed her womb" (v. 5).

Hannah's grief was provoked by Peninnah (see v. 6). Can you imagine? Maybe you have experience with someone knowing your deepest hurt and using it to provoke and irritate you, to deliberately put you down.

DO WE SUFFER BECAUSE OF OUR ANCESTORS?

Let's unpack this. This story may cause you to feel an array of emotions—sadness for Hannah, annoyance with Peninnah, compassion, and confusion. (Two wives? How does that work?) You may also feel anger toward the Lord. Again, emotions are not sinful, but how we react with those emotions can be sinful.

Whether from compassion or curiosity, you may wonder why God closed the womb of a faithful woman like Hannah. Some of the people around her believed she brought this on herself, that she or an ancestor had some secret sin and now God was punishing her.

People have this same response to sad situations today. A terminal illness, a sudden death, or a baby's disorder sometimes spark comments along the lines of "It must run in the family." Scripture seems to support this:

> Our fathers sinned, and are no more; and we bear their iniquities. (Lamentations 5:7)

> For I the LORD your God am a jealous God, visiting the iniquity of the fathers on the children to the third and the fourth generation of those who hate Me, but showing steadfast love to thousands of those who love Me and keep My commandments. (Exodus 20:5–6)

But we must be careful about using these passages out of context. Do we inherit sin? Absolutely. We are all born sinful due to the fall of mankind in Genesis 3. Can the sins of our family cause us to sin too? Yes. For example, a study conducted over sixteen years found that child abuse and neglect had a direct effect on adult partner violence perpetration. It also found that being abused or neglected as a child is a predictor for juvenile violence.[17] But let's look more closely at this. Is the child who is being neglected and harmed at fault? Their parents sinned in this way, and perhaps their grandparents did too. Is that what this means? Can you see where that thinking leaves us feeling heartbroken and invalidated, and

MYTH 6: PRAY HARDER

perhaps causes us to judge or cast shame on the victim? Friend, may this be a reminder that taking the Bible out of context can be harmful.

Such thinking is a type of theology called cause and effect. For example, a believer may think that present trouble is God's punishment for past sin. But this is Law-oriented and ignores the Gospel. Jesus took the wrath of our sins when He died on the cross for us. He fulfilled the Law for us. Now God looks at us through the mercy and grace of His Son.

It's true that we are subject to the Law and must often bear the consequences of our actions. For example, the thief on the cross was crucified for his crime. But the Gospel message for us is that Jesus redeemed him. His faith in Jesus as the Savior means he is spending eternity in heaven.

Back to Hannah. In 1 Samuel, see that throughout her years of barrenness, despite years of unanswered prayer, God used the experience to refine her faith and strengthen her before blessing her with the gift of Samuel. In response, Hannah spoke from a place of heartfelt faith and gratitude. She lifted up the one thing she held most dear, her beloved child, and said, "I will give him to the Lord all the days of his life" (1 Samuel 1:11). God worked through this time of waiting and frustration to bring Hannah closer to Himself. She surrendered to His will, not her own. She wasn't saying, "Give me a son because I want one." Rather, she petitioned, with her whole heart, that if God would remember her, she would give that gift right back to Him.

Do we have something in our lives we desperately want or need? I think back to some of my prayers, my petitions. Did I yield them to the Lord, ending them by saying, "Your will be done"? Not always. Especially the ones that were too hard to verbalize—the soaked pillow prayers that I struggled to even pray. That's because I worried that God's will wasn't what I wanted. What if His answer is for my loved one to be in heaven with Him?

WE ARE NOT DEFINED BY OUR PAST

One of the best-known accounts of transformation from a life of sin to a life of ministry is that of Paul, first known as Saul, in the New Testament. Saul was committed to his understanding of religious zeal and rabbinical law to the extent that he was famous for imprisoning or even killing people who followed Jesus of Nazareth.

> **Still breathing threats and murder against the disciples of the Lord, . . . he approached Damascus, and suddenly a light from heaven shone around him. And falling to the ground, he heard a voice saying to him, "Saul, Saul, why are you persecuting Me?" And he said, "Who are You, Lord?" And He said, "I am Jesus, whom you are persecuting. But rise and enter the city, and you will be told what you are to do."** (Acts 9:1, 3-6)

Blinded, Saul was led into Damascus and "neither ate nor drank" for three days (v. 9). Then, the believer Ananias laid hands on him and spoke. Afterward, "something like scales fell from his eyes, and he regained his sight. Then he rose and was baptized; and taking food, he was strengthened" (vv. 18-19). Jesus confronted Saul and converted him to a believer. Saul immediately began to proclaim Jesus as the Son of God (see v. 20).

What a testimony! A man who was well-known for targeting Christians for persecution not only believed in Christ but was completely and unapologetically vocal that Jesus is the Son of God. Saul's past was a part of him, and God used that past to bring glory to Himself. God's grace refined Saul, now Paul, to be one of Christianity's most significant missionaries and to be a prolific writer of the New Testament.

Our world wants our past to become our identity. Research shows that people who experience trauma often struggle to overcome it to the point that it affects their identity.[18] While our past impacts us, our true identity is in the One who has overcome our past and now saves us.

God can use our story, our past or present trauma, to shape us and bless others, ultimately glorifying God. Yes, I know, if you're in the middle of your storm, that's not the answer you want to hear, but I pray that the Holy Spirit works through these words to comfort you. Even at our worst moments, God can draw us closer. Do you remember the saying "When you find yourself in these obstacles, and you've fallen of your back, the only way you can look is up" from earlier in this book?

MYTH 6: PRAY HARDER

When I first heard that saying, our family's trauma hadn't happened yet, but I knew people who had gone through difficult things, and I was angry for them. I wanted to shout, "How can horrible things make us grow closer to Jesus?!" Now, of course, "we know that for those who love God all things work together for good, for those who are called according to His purpose" (Romans 8:28). He can use the horrific moments to work through the people and the situation to draw us closer to Him. When everything collapses around us, we can see that we are not surviving of our own accord but because of God's strength in us.

> **And after you have suffered a little while, the God of all grace, who has called you to His eternal glory in Christ, will Himself restore, confirm, strengthen, and establish you.** (1 Peter 5:10)

BE A WITNESS

Before we look at examples in our own lives where we can witness for Christ, let's look at Acts 16:22–34, which recounts when Paul and Silas were in prison. Paul was no stranger to jail, but this place was a torture chamber, probably a dungeon or a cave, and the jailer was free to restrain prisoners however he chose.

> **The crowd joined in attacking them, and the magistrates tore the garments off them and gave orders to beat them with rods. And when they had inflicted many blows upon them, they threw them into prison, ordering the jailer to keep them safely. Having received this order, he put them into the inner prison and fastened their feet in the stocks.** (Acts 16:22-24)

So, they were suffering, that's for sure. But we find them singing and praising the Lord and praying, which is exactly what landed them in prison in the first place. And other "prisoners were listening to them" (v. 25)! An earthquake came, and the doors were opened and the chains were unfastened (v. 26). The jailer saw this and was about to kill himself because he thought the prisoners had escaped. (Back then, if your prisoner escaped, the jailer could be executed for dereliction of duty.) Paul and Silas told him to stop because all the prisoners were still there. By this time, the jailer had heard them sing and praise God, even in their suffering. What an experience that would have been for the jailer and other prisoners! The jailer wanted more; he wanted to be saved. Paul told him how:

> And they said, "Believe in the Lord Jesus, and you will be saved, you and your household." And they spoke the word of the Lord to him and to all who were in his house. And he took them the same hour of the night and washed their wounds; and he was baptized at once, he and all his family. Then he brought them up into his house and set food before them. And he rejoiced along with his entire household that he had believed in God. (Acts 16:31–34)

In the middle of their suffering, by the work of the Holy Spirit, Paul and Silas witnessed about Jesus to those around them. The entire trajectory of that family and the offspring of that family was changed. This story of the jailer's conversion and Baptism into God's family is packed with important lessons. The one I encourage you to think about now is that because of the Holy Spirit working through Paul and Silas, their hymns and prayers in the midst of their trials, they were a testimony for God to others around them.

Let me give you a few more examples of God using our worst moments and turning them around for our good. We'll start small.

Maybe you work in an environment that is toxic. This could be unhealthy communication, microaggressions, ostracism, disrespect, or even harassment. I believe all of us have a story or know of someone who has experienced these things and more. We hear these stories and wonder why would God allow it. Yet because of those moments and those stories, we have a culture that is trying to remedy that. You hear of Wellness Wednesdays where you can partake in a healthy exercise on the company's dime. You hear of management being trained in strategies for healthy communication. You hear of people going off and starting their own company with the determination to be different and be a healthy, effective company, not like the one they worked in before they started their own. God took a situation that was more than likely filled with frustration and turmoil and used it to bless people through a new company or a new policy.

MYTH 6: PRAY HARDER

Another way that God uses our sufferings and frustrations is by refining our faith and sharpening us. When we pray our prayers, sometimes God will use uncomfortable situations to grow us. For example, I'm someone who likes to be a people pleaser. I will do all I can to make sure everyone around me is feeling good and isn't upset with me. Is there a conflict? Yeah, I'll be walking the other way. I've struggled with this and have prayed that God would help me overcome that way of thinking so I can truly rest in how He defines me: "Fearfully and wonderfully made" (Psalm 139:14).

As I prayed this, I didn't understand why God would allow uncomfortable situations and moments when I cried to my therapist, "I don't understand what I did wrong." I couldn't understand why God would allow more stress in my life. Why would He allow someone to be cruel and unkind? Yet looking back, I see my growth happened through those things. It made me lean on what God, not someone else, speaks about me. It made me understand more fully that I cannot control everything and everyone, even if my sinful mind believes I can. I found myself clinging to God's Word through the Psalms and in prayer to help me navigate a time when I often felt unworthy and unloved.

Lastly, I think of my personal story and my trauma. Again, I'll never fully understand why my cousin was killed. Some answers won't come until we can ask God face to face. But this tragic, unthinkable situation was a time that He used for His good plan. What Satan wanted to destroy, God used to bless others. For example, my faith could have been shaken and I could have fallen away from Christ. Yet it drew our family closer and made my relationship with Christ stronger. Our family knows a pain that is hard to verbalize. Yet when we meet someone who feels the pain of loss, we can connect over our own painful experiences. Our family can be a witness for Christ by sharing our story with others who have faced similar hardships. We have partnered with organizations to bring awareness to the harms of technology and the evils of this world. We are able to relate to others, and we have the same questions fueling our sighs and memories of small moments with our loved ones. And we have the same promise of eternity with Jesus.

Back to Hannah. How many parents have read that account, prayed that prayer, and felt seen and heard, then loved a long-awaited baby?

Hannah's story is still comforting people so much thousands of years later. God wants us to be in community with one another. Through our pain and turmoil, God calls us closer to one another, seen and heard, and brings us closer to Him. This happens in brief interpersonal interactions, when we participate in a prayer chain, and when we come together to worship, singing hymns, confessing our faith in the words of the Apostles' Creed, praying in unison, and kneeling shoulder to shoulder at the Lord's Supper.

Finally, we look at 1 Corinthians 4:12–13:

We labor, working with our own hands. When reviled, we bless; when persecuted, we endure; when slandered, we entreat. We have become, and are still, like the scum of the earth, the refuse of all things.

We will have moments of frustration and pain when this world treats us unkindly. Yet as Christians, we are in this world but not of this world. We speak the Gospel with our words and actions. Paul again reminds us that we will be slandered and will experience persecution. This is not a matter of if but when. May we respond as he did, with hymns, prayers, and faith in God's deliverance.

WE ARE THE CREATURES, NOT THE CREATOR

As we consider further why bad things happen, we need to recognize that we may never know the answer. We can discuss and ponder, we can give the Sunday School answer of sin, but there are times when we will be left wondering why.

Here is a phrase that has helped me with this myth: "We are the creatures, and God is the Creator." As a creature, we don't know everything God is doing or why. We can wonder, ruminate, study, and analyze, but unless the Lord determines to reveal the answer, we just may never know. While it's not the most profound or scholarly answer, it is an answer that is rooted in trust that goodness comes from God. Our capacity to trust is limited by our sinfulness, but we can rest in the promise of eternal life with God in heaven and the joy of the resurrection.

What shocks us is the evil of this world. Our hearts ache at the suffering

MYTH 6: PRAY HARDER

that sin has caused. Yet because we are witnesses to these sins, we are given a front-row seat to the need for the Gospel. When bad things happen to us or our loved ones, we can draw deeply from the Word of God and witness to others the love of Jesus and promise of eternity in heaven where sin and shame are no more.

We see this example in the story of Jesus and the woman in Luke 8. This woman had an issue—a period gone wrong for twelve years. This made her unclean, according to Jewish law. No one could sit where she sat or touch what she touched. The woman was ostracized. And no one, including doctors, could figure out what was wrong and heal her (see v. 43). The woman, who had heard of Jesus and the miracles He was working for people, put her faith in Him. Since she was unclean, she had to be surreptitious about getting close to Him. A brief touch of the fringe of His garment was all she needed (see v. 44). And Jesus didn't let the moment go unnoticed. He called her out in front of everyone! He did not chastise her for breaking the rules or for sneaking in behind Him. He publicly acknowledged her faith. What an incredible moment for that crowd to see! And what a moment when Jesus reassured that woman that He loved her and made her pure.

We see something similar in the account of Jesus and the Samaritan woman in John 4. As He and His disciples were traveling on a hot day, Jesus stopped at the well to drink at the same time that a Samaritan woman came to draw water (see v. 7). They were there in the middle of the day, which was not the regular time to draw water. She was there at that time because she was an outcast. She had multiple husbands and was currently living with a man she wasn't married to (see v. 18). Yet here was Jesus, in a place that Jewish people avoided, talking to an unaccompanied woman in public. What was more, a Jewish man talking to a Samaritan woman simply was not done. In this remarkable conversation, Jesus revealed Himself to be the Messiah for the first time: "I who speak to you am He" (v. 26). Fully aware of the significance of that statement, "the woman left her water jar and went away into town and said to the people, 'Come, see a man who told me all that I ever did. Can this be the Christ?' They went out of the town and were coming to Him" (v. 28–30).

This powerful account shows how much Jesus changes our hearts. He took a woman who was so outcast that she wasn't even in the same place at the same time as other women, and He spoke to her a message of the promise fulfilled.

As Christians, we can be assured that when it seems the floor has fallen out beneath us, Jesus is with us. We may not "feel" Him, but accounts like these are our proof. To be honest, when my family's tragedy was uncovered, I didn't feel Him. Yet God worked through my husband to support and comfort me and remind me of God's mercy and grace. Friend, Jesus is with us in the level two pains and in the level ten pains. He hears our prayers and works through people such as family, friends, therapists, and pastors to provide comfort, companionship, and reminders that God truly works through all things for us.

MAY WE GIVE THANKS AND PRAISE

As we wrap up this chapter and topic, let us finish with praise:

My praise is continually of You. (Psalm 71:6)

We praise Him for never forsaking us. We praise Him for providing support from those around us and through unexpected people or places. We praise Him for sustaining us through some of the worst hurt we may ever feel. Lastly, we praise Him that He loved us so much He watched His own Son be betrayed, tortured, ridiculed, mocked, and crucified so that we could have eternal life with Him in heaven. God knows our pains and our hurts because He watched His own Son go through it too.

We tend to turn inward and be so self-focused that we think we are the only ones suffering or that God can't possibly understand our pain and turmoil. But God does. He is right there with us through it all and reminds us that through His Son, Jesus, one day, there will be no pain. There will be no suffering. One day, we will be in heaven.

And do not be grieved, for the joy of the Lord is your strength. (Nehemiah 8:10)

MYTH 6: PRAY HARDER

We won't have all the answers in this life. Some things will remain a mystery until all is revealed to us in heaven. For now, we can be certain of His faithfulness to us, certain of His grace because of what He has done for us by His death and resurrection.

For that, I will praise God. I will praise Him that He has used horrific events in my life and frustrations big and small to bring me closer to Him. He has worked all those things together for my good. Lastly, He has provided a solution to the sin of this world through His Son, Jesus.

PRAYER:

Lord God,
Thank You for never forsaking me. While so often I feel like David, crying out that I feel hidden from You, I never am. Because of sin, we face unexpected evil and hurt, but You, God, have provided blessings throughout those hurts and an everlasting hope to sustain us through them in Your promise of eternal life. Thank You. I pray that You continue to work all things together for our good. Help me to be a blessing to others who may be experiencing the same sufferings I face and continue to refine my faith, bringing me closer to You.
In Jesus' name. Amen.

GENTLE REMINDERS:

- Everything bad is a result of sin.
- Even in our worst moments, God will not leave us.
- God can use moments of pain to help refine our faith, bring us closer to Him, and help us witness our faith to others.
- We can praise God for His continual faithfulness.

JOURNAL PROMPT:

What is a pillow-soaking moment for you? Do you struggle to understand it? What can you release to God for Him to carry? How can you share your testimony with someone?

MYTH 7
OTHERS HAVE IT WORSE

"Don't cry about it; be grateful."

"Quit complaining."

"It's not that bad. Get over it."

We are in the thick of our bedtime routine with our two- and four-year-olds. Baths that flood the floor, toddlers running back and forth from bedroom to bedroom, burning energy left from the day. We settle down and read three books. No more, no less. Then we pray.

Our routine starts with the Lord's Prayer, continues with a classic bedtime prayer that resonates with my childhood, and wraps up with a little "end prayer," as my grandma Joan would call it. Each night, we take turns leading this end prayer. Tonight is my daughter's turn: "Dear Jesus, please be with Mommy, Daddy, Lydia, and Ezekiel. Jesus, be with all of us if we are scared of thunder, monsters, and bad guys. Amen."

She pauses, looks at us with her piercing blue eyes, tilts her head, and asks, "What are you scared of?"

My husband and I were taken aback. Our eyes connected, and my mind turned. *How do we answer this? Do we acknowledge that Mommy and Daddy get scared too? Are we honest, but not so much that we add to her fears?*

Finally, we resort to saying, "Thunder." In her innocence, she responds with, "Oh, me too. And monsters. Are you scared of monsters?" Yep, Baby Girl, we are. Are they the kind of monsters she thinks about? No. These are adult monsters. The monsters of death, of not being able to make ends meet, of injustice, of health problems. Monsters of evil.

We all have such monsters, even if we don't name them aloud.

MYTH 7: OTHERS HAVE IT WORSE

(Because if we say it, we are admitting it exists.) We are having to confront the thing that wants to stay in the dark and drag us there too. Just you and the monster. This is where Satan likes us to be—hidden away from hope, where the darkness absorbs light and where our mind battles alone.

Sometimes, we work up the courage and, with sweaty palms and racing hearts, share the monster. If you've ever done that, I commend you. It can be so hard to expose that monster to daylight. We may stumble over the words or keep some of it hidden, yet we share. We open ourselves to slaying the monster, to safe resolution.

SAFE VERSUS UNSAFE

Two things can happen when we expose our monster to daylight. The person we talk with is a trusted friend, pastor, counselor, or mentor who responds with affirmation, compassion, and Christ-centered words that guide us toward the assurances of Scripture. This is a healthy interaction that sets things in motion to reduce or remove the monster.

Or the person we talk with wants to help, wants to comfort us, wants to give us perspective. They truly have our best interests at heart and don't want us to feel insignificant. But they want a quick fix for us. And they remind us that "other people have it worse." "At least it's not (fill in the blank)." "I know you're upset, but it isn't that bad."

If you want to invalidate someone and make them feel like a small ant on top of a massive mountain, then say something like that. You probably *don't* want someone you care about to feel this way, but maybe you have said something like this without knowing the effect the words can have. I said things like this often before I truly understood the pain such sayings can cause. To be frank, I think no one really understands until they walk through their own trial and someone says it to them. That's how it was for me. After several people said these kind but detrimental words, I wanted to scream, "NO! That's not helping." I know now that a healthy reaction would have been to let people know that this phrase in particular brought me to tears and did not bring me comfort. It's okay to let people know, in a respectful way, that something upsets you.

You may be thinking, *Okay, Faith. I can see how that invalidates a person, but what can I do instead? How can I honor the person who is sharing her vulnerabilities and lead her to the One who carries the hurt, pain, and grief?* Well, friend, let's open our Bibles and find out together.

Helpful moment: Earlier, I wrote about sharing vulnerability with a safe person. I just want to take a beat and go over what makes a person safe or unsafe, helpful or harmful. This applies to when you are this for someone and when someone is being this for you. If you're like me, you've confessed sins and shared thoughts with someone who did not have your best interest at heart. This may have led to more turmoil instead of Jesus and healing. In any case, I pray these thoughts help you as much as they did me when I first learned them.

A Safe Person

promotes connection;

gives us grace, unconditional love, and acceptance with no condemnation;

speaks the truth; and

is honest.

An Unsafe Person

doesn't admit weaknesses;

is self-righteous;

demands trust instead of earning it;

blames others;

betrays your confidence;

lies; and

has all the answers (is a know-it-all).

Interpersonal Traits of Unsafe People

They avoid closeness instead of connecting.

They are only concerned about "I" instead of "we."

MYTH 7: OTHERS HAVE IT WORSE

They flatter us instead of confronting us.

They condemn us instead of forgiving us.

They stay in parent or child roles instead of relating as equals.

They are inconsistent.

They are a negative influence rather than a positive one.

Friend, we all are sinners and all fall short, so if we do not respond to someone in a helpful, comforting, Christ-centered way, we can ask for forgiveness and change how we engage with that person. We can still use discernment before we share our hearts with others. I pray you use these points to help guide you to safe people and help you be a safe confidant for others.

LEADING WITH COMPASSION, NOT JUDGMENT

The Holy Spirit works through the Word of God, through the Sacraments, and through other people in our lives to remind us that Jesus sees us and loves us. Each time we receive the Lord's Supper, the Spirit refreshes us and strengthens our faith. This sacrament is Jesus coming to us in person. The Spirit renews the gifts of our Baptism daily. It's important to remember that this renewal and strengthening is not something we do ourselves—it comes to us from the work of the Holy Spirit.

> **So we do not lose heart. Though our outer self is wasting away, our inner self is being renewed day by day. For this light momentary affliction is preparing us for an eternal weight of glory beyond all comparison.** (2 Corinthians 4:16–17)

In the Bible, Jesus is our model for how to be a community, a comfort, and a listening ear to those around us. Let's look at a few examples.

In Matthew 9, Jesus had spent many days teaching and "healing every disease and every affliction" (v. 35). Matthew tells us that Jesus saw the crowds and had compassion for them. He saw people afflicted with disease and hurt who were "harassed and helpless" (v. 36). As word about Him spread, people flocked to Him. While we don't know much about these people, we can imagine some may have created some of their own problems. And how did Jesus respond to the crowds? He didn't tell them to just pray more or try harder. He didn't tell them to deal with it because "God only gives us what we can handle."

Jesus led with compassion. He led with understanding and comfort. And as the end of Matthew 9 and the beginning of Matthew 10 tell us, Jesus called His disciples to extend compassion and care to the hurting. Friend, we can do this too. When someone we love comes to us with heartache and need, God calls and empowers us to respond with compassion.

Another story like this is the feeding of the five thousand. In John 5, we read that Jesus' power and authority are from God the Father. And in John 6, we read that Jesus was followed by a large crowd (see vv. 1–2). Again, He responded with compassion, this time providing for their immediate physical need. "Where are we to buy bread, so that these people may eat?" (v. 5).

By His divine nature, Jesus knew the answer but wanted to make the point with His disciples. We know what happened next: after much talk, one of the disciples found a boy with five barley loaves and two fish—enough for one meal for one child. Then, in this public place where thousands could see and benefit from His divinity, Jesus gave thanks and multiplied the food so the whole assembly was provided for (see vv. 9–12). What's more, by the hand of God the Son, through the work of the disciples, every person there had as much as they wanted—and more!

What about us? When someone comes to us with a burden or a trial, do we slyly look at the clock to see how long the conversation will take? Do we brush them off so we can do something more interesting? Or do we show compassion like Jesus did? In the account of the feeding of the five thousand, Jesus put the crowd's needs before His own and gave them what they needed in that moment. The takeaway for us is that sometimes we may be called upon to address someone's need before we can continue on with our own work. But note that we are on the receiving end of Jesus' abundant provision. He looks on us with compassion and gives us what we need.

MYTH 7: OTHERS HAVE IT WORSE

LET'S BE THERE FOR ONE ANOTHER
AND SHARE OUR BURDENS

When we're going through a tough time, being surrounded by people we love makes a big difference in how we handle it. The account of Naomi and Ruth is an example. Naomi, who was grieving the loss of her husband and two sons, wanted to go back to Bethlehem, where her family would provide for her. Her sons' wives would go home to their families for the same reason. It didn't make sense to her that her daughters-in-law would come with her instead of returning to their own families, so Naomi told them to return to their parents' homes (see Ruth 1:11). Ruth disagreed: "Do not urge me to leave you or to return from following you. For where you go I will go, and where you lodge I will lodge" (v. 16). Ruth stayed true to her loyalty to her mother-in-law and showed us that even when people push us away because they may be feeling grief and sadness, we can stay with them to bring them comfort, with the help of the Holy Spirit working through us.

The Gospels tell us that Jesus often stopped what He was doing and ministered to people in the moment. The woman at the well (John 4:1–42), the woman with the issue of blood (Mark 5:25–34), Jairus's daughter (Mark 5:21–43), the widow of Nain (Luke 7:11–17), Bartimaeus (Mark 10:46–52) . . . The list goes on and on. Jesus called the disciples to minister in His name. And He calls us as well. In John 15:12, He tells us how we are to interact with one another: "This is My commandment, that you love one another as I have loved you."

This love is evidenced by His humility—God the Son coming to us as an infant—and His teaching, preaching, healing, working miracles, suffering, and dying to take on the weight of our sin. We will never reach that level of selflessness, but we can treat one another with kindness, thoughtfulness, and compassion. We can respond with grace and empathy when someone in need comes to us. And we can do all this in the name of Christ Jesus.

The flip side of this is that just as we show love to one another, we receive that love too. We are called to share our burdens. Galatians 6:2

tells us to "bear one another's burdens, and so fulfill the law of Christ." We cannot bear one another's burdens if we do not reach out to others in the first place. God didn't call for us to process these emotions and interactions alone. He gave us a community of believers to help us navigate it all.

> **Blessed are those who mourn, for they shall be comforted.** (Matthew 5:4)

> **[God] comforts us in all our affliction, so that we may be able to comfort those who are in any affliction, with the comfort with which we ourselves are comforted by God.** (2 Corinthians 1:4)

> **Rejoice with those who rejoice; weep with those who weep.** (Romans 12:15)

Jesus showed us this in action after the death of Lazarus:

> **When Jesus saw her weeping, and the Jews who had come with her also weeping, He was deeply moved in His spirit and greatly troubled. And He said, "Where have you laid him?" They said to Him, "Lord, come and see." Jesus wept.** (John 11:33–35)

Again, "Jesus *wept*." Jesus knew in advance that He would restore Lazarus to life. He knew He would perform this miracle to show His own divine power over death and to bring glory to God. But when He saw how sad His friends were because they had no hope, He cried with them. How amazing is that? Jesus shows us the importance of just being with His friends in their pain, to show up and to connect with them.

Our God of all comfort promises to work through the people around us to help soothe our pain during our times of sorrow. This moves us to be with others in the midst of their grief and struggle. When we sit with them, we are not distracting them with sayings like "Others have it worse" or trying to shift their perspective to how bad things could be. Instead, we mourn with them. We cry with them and comfort them. We assist them in whatever ways we are able. And we remind them of the promises of Jesus in Scripture.

MYTH 7: OTHERS HAVE IT WORSE

ARE WE ENCOURAGING OR DISCOURAGING?

A great place to go for a lesson on how to encourage others is the account of Job. We looked at his life in chapter 4, but another part of his story that applies here is Job's friends.

First, let's refresh. At the start, Job had everything: wife, kids, money, livestock, property; you name it, and this guy had it. Then, God allowed Satan to attack Job, and he lost everything. Yep, everything.

Later, his three friends, Eliphaz, Bildad, and Zophar, came to talk with him (see Job 2:11). They started off comforting him and showing sympathy: "They sat with him on the ground, seven days and seven nights, and no one spoke a word to him, for they saw that his suffering was very great" (v. 13).

A lesson for us here is this: just sit with your loved one. Sit. Cry. Be present. Pray. So often, we believe we need to fill the silence. We feel like we should say the right thing or do the best thing, but sometimes the best comfort is just our presence. Job's three friends did just that. They didn't ask him tons of questions or tell him to get over it. They didn't tell him to go back to work and earn it all back. They just sat and allowed the Holy Spirit to work through the silence.

After those seven days, when Job started complaining, then his three friends felt they needed to answer. They started taking turns. Instead of just being present with him to listen and pray, they did the opposite. In chapters 4 and 5, Job's friend Eliphaz ended up just adding to his misery. Eliphaz told Job that it was his fault: "For affliction does not come from the dust, nor does trouble sprout from the ground" (Job 5:6). Long-winded Eliphaz told Job many things that on the surface were true but proved only that Eliphaz was a judgmental friend who thought that if Job had only prayed harder or been a better person, his problems wouldn't have existed.

Friend, this is an easy posture to take. We listen and commiserate and hang around. But sometimes we are tempted to say "If only you had . . ." in an attempt to put the situation in the past. Instead, let us truly listen, ask compassionate questions, recognize the other person's pain as valid, and humble ourselves.

GOD'S ENCOURAGING WORD

Just like we learned in chapter 6, there are many reasons hard things happen, and while it can be healthy to work through those thoughts, that work may have to happen with the assistance of mental health professionals and pastoral care. When we are called on to offer comfort to our loved ones, it's okay to just be present.

MAY WE LAMENT

The account of Job and his friends shows us a lot of what not to do when someone we love is hurting. Now you may be wondering what we can or should do.

The book of Lamentations can guide us as we dive into this topic more. Jeremiah, the author of Lamentations, was God's "iron" prophet (Jeremiah 1:18). God sent him to rebuke the people of Judah. Jeremiah spent the majority of his days rebuking people and prophesying that a punishment would come. Talk about a rough job. Imagine day in and day out telling people, "You are a sinner, and you just keep sinning! You turned your back on God. Your sin will destroy you. But God does not want to turn His back on you. Repent!"

Lamentations is a short book written after that punishment came and Jerusalem lay destroyed and in rubble. It communicates that even faithful Jeremiah struggled with the pain and suffering that sin causes. Jeremiah is not alone, of course. You or a loved one may be walking a hard path right now. It can be easy for us to try to suppress our feelings and pretend that all is dandy regarding our relationship with God. In the complaint psalms (e.g., Psalms 6; 44; 74; 79; 88; 90; 102), Jeremiah and David show us that we can cry out to God, confess our sins, voice our complaints, and generally rail against the Lord. Our Creator knows what is in our hearts and knows our thoughts before we even think them. He is a witness to our sin and the trouble sin causes. We can be honest with Him.

WHAT IS LAMENT? HOW CAN WE DO IT?

It's okay to lament—to pray with all the sorrow and anguish and confusion we feel. We don't even have to use our own words to pray this

MYTH 7: OTHERS HAVE IT WORSE

way. Some of the psalms express deep sorrow and anguish. Psalm 13, for example, shows us how David worked through his feelings, calling out to God: "How long, O LORD? Will You forget me forever? How long will You hide Your face from me?" (v. 1). David asked God how long he would have to suffer and begged God to "consider and answer me . . . light up my eyes" (v. 3).

We can pray to God and for whatever we need at that moment. Do we need comfort? wisdom? guidance? patience? deliverance?

After unburdening his heart, David yielded everything to God and praised Him:

> But I have trusted in Your steadfast love; my heart shall rejoice in Your salvation. I will sing to the LORD, because He has dealt bountifully with me. (vv. 5–6)

David reminded himself of the good God has already done for him. He voiced his trust in God, who had "dealt bountifully" and promised salvation. This is how David could bring himself to rejoice.

Friend, we can lean on David's example and words when someone we love is going through a hard time. We can sit with them, help them recognize and name their suffering and the emotions they are feeling. We can pray for them and with them and ask that God provide what they need—peace, comfort, hope, and the assurance of forgiveness and salvation.

Finally, when the world tells us to rely on ourselves, to just try harder, we can instead yield all of our worries to God, confident that He will work all together for our good, just as Paul tells us in Romans 8:28:

> And we know that for those who love God all things work together for good, for those who are called according to His purpose.

GOD SHOWS US HIS CHARACTER

The process of lamenting, praying, and trusting in God's mercy can be hard, but through it, the triune God shows us His character and His love for us. We turn to His Word to be reminded again and again about God's character:

> This God—His way is perfect; the word of the LORD proves true; He is a shield for all those who take refuge in Him. (Psalm 18:30)
>
> This is the message we have heard from Him and proclaim to you, that God is light, and in Him is no darkness at all. (1 John 1:5)
>
> For the word of God is living and active, sharper than any two-edged sword, piercing to the division of soul and of spirit, of joints and of marrow, and discerning the thoughts and intentions of the heart. (Hebrews 4:12)

The Bible shows us again and again who God is and that He is constant, unchanging, faithful, and merciful. God's Word is alive and active within us, giving us wisdom and guidance as we navigate our thoughts and actions. The more we turn to the Bible to see God's character, the more He reveals that character to us.

> Look at the birds of the air: they neither sow nor reap nor gather into barns, and yet your heavenly Father feeds them. Are you not of more value than they? (Matthew 6:26)
>
> Every good gift and every perfect gift is from above, coming down from the Father of lights, with whom there is no variation or shadow due to change. (James 1:17)

We can trust God, we can rest in His protection, and we can remember that He will always love us and never forsake us:

> Be strong and courageous. Do not fear or be in dread of them, for it is the LORD your God who goes with you. He will not leave you or forsake you. (Deuteronomy 31:6)

IS IT OKAY IF WE SHOW GRATITUDE?

The saying "Others have it worse" (and others like it) does a lot more harm than good. It invalidates people, instead of encouraging them, and distances them, instead of drawing them closer. Yet is there a small lesson we can still learn from these words? I think so.

In his complaint psalms, David often went from asking, "God, did You forget me?" to remembering that God has given him so much and singing praises to the Lord.

MYTH 7: OTHERS HAVE IT WORSE

During the depths of despair and pain, it can be hard to see the sliver of joy. Our days can be like a dark cloud that hides the light. But Scripture reminds us of the light of Christ that we have by faith. That light may look like a hot meal from a friend, a note from a relative, a sunrise seen from a hospital window, or a hug.

Friend, it's okay to both cry out to God in pain and suffering and to praise Him for all His benefits to us. Psalm 62:8 reminds us,

Trust in Him at all times, O people; pour out your hearts before Him; God is a refuge for us.

God is our refuge, our shelter and protection from danger or distress. We know that God is on our side:

The LORD is on my side; I will not fear. What can man do to me? (Psalm 118:6)

Jesus tells us to expect life to be hard:

I have said these things to you, that in Me you may have peace. In the world you will have tribulation. But take heart; I have overcome the world. (John 16:33)

It can't be said often enough that we have Jesus, who has overcome the world. No amount of suffering can remove us from the love of God and the hope that we find in Jesus' death and resurrection.

WE DON'T HAVE A SCOREBOARD

This scene might be familiar to you: When one person shares her burdens and worries, another person responds with her own burdens and worries. People match problem for problem, piling on until someone gives. Or the scene is one-sided. One person spills her heart, and the listener, who has legitimate issues of her own, says nothing because she doesn't want to be compared to anyone or she shared too much last week or she's too embarrassed.

It's like there's a sorrow scoreboard. That's when we compare our walks of life with those around us. Friend, there is no scoreboard. Everyone has heartache of some kind. And as we've established, sharing our concerns can be healthy when we yield all of our anxieties at Jesus' feet, rely on His mercy, and seek His will for our lives.

We do not need to compare our grief and trials, but we don't need to hide them either. We can rejoice in the glory that is Christ. We can use these moments to remember God's provision and protection, His grace and love for us in Christ.

GRACE IS OUR EXAMPLE

In 2 Corinthians 12:9–10, Paul tells us this:

But He said to me, "My grace is sufficient for you, for My power is made perfect in weakness." Therefore I will boast all the more gladly of my weaknesses, so that the power of Christ may rest upon me. For the sake of Christ, then, I am content with weaknesses, insults, hardships, persecutions, and calamities. For when I am weak, then I am strong.

What beautiful words! Jesus' grace is enough for us. We don't need more than what He can and will give us.

Hebrews 4:15–16 says,

For we do not have a high priest who is unable to sympathize with our weaknesses, but one who in every respect has been tempted as we are, yet without sin. Let us then with confidence draw near to the throne of grace, that we may receive mercy and find grace to help in time of need.

Jesus was human. You may have heard the words "true man." He was tempted, just like us. He wept, just like we do. Through Jesus, we have mercy and grace to sustain us.

This is the message we can communicate to our loved ones, not words like "Other people have it worse, so quit complaining." We can come alongside people in their sorrow and point them to the grace and peace that is only found in Christ Jesus.

MYTH 7: OTHERS HAVE IT WORSE

PRAYER:

Heavenly Father,
Thank You for providing us with a way to bring our concerns, our worries, and our fears to You through the death and resurrection of Your Son, Jesus. Thank You for providing us a community of loved ones who want to support us, comfort us, and help us on the journeys that we walk through on this side of heaven. Thank You for giving us the gift of lamenting. Lord, we ask that You continue to strengthen us as we bring those anxieties to You. Give us discernment and show us who are safe and unsafe people in our lives for us to share our vulnerabilities with. Lastly, may we look to You and trust Your will for us as we share our burdens with others and make decisions that bring glory to You and Your kingdom.
In Jesus' name. Amen.

GENTLE REMINDERS:

- Discern who a safe person is to share your vulnerabilities with.
- Lead with compassion, not judgment, when others share with you.
- Lament to God.
- Remember God's character and His promises to you.
- Share burdens with one another.
- Don't compare your pain points to others. Everyone's is valid.

JOURNAL PROMPT:

Who is a safe person in your life? Why? What do you need to lament to God right now? What can you set at His feet and release? Whom could you reach out to to be a listening ear for?

MYTH 8
BE YOUR OWN HERO

"You go do you, boo!"

"Be your own _____."

"If it is to be, it is up to me."

"I can do it on my own."

"Faith, remove the cape." I was on a Zoom call with my therapist, talking about how I had so much to do and so little time. I poured out my frustrations: I was overwhelmed and felt despair at not being able to do everything as well as I wanted to. My dear therapist, whom God is working through, looked at me with compassion and said, "Faith, remove the cape. The superwoman cape is doing it all. It's not yours to carry." Her words changed my perspective, and I realized that I can't do everything on my own.

Has someone said something like that to you? Did a light bulb go off in your head?

"A good Christian doesn't need help with household chores."

"A good Christian doesn't need to have alone time. They should be with their kids, at all times, and enjoy it."

"A good Christian . . ." Insert the phrase you've heard here.

We want to believe these myths. It's exciting to think we can go it on our own. It's empowering to imagine ourselves accomplishing every goal and dream without help. But this is impossible.

During the pandemic, our world had to remove the idea of community from daily life. For a while, we had to rely on our favorite restaurants to deliver meals to our doorsteps. Need groceries or toiletries? Order

MYTH 8: BE YOUR OWN HERO

through an app and pick them up without having to get out of your car. Are you sick? Log in to your portal for a telehealth visit. No direct human interaction necessary.

Technology is a wonderful thing and a benefit to everyone, but in our postpandemic world, we should not live outside the range of support and assistance from others and rely on these things too much, which is the opposite of the type of community God created us for.

At the root of these phrases and the idea that we can do it all by ourselves is idolatry. Satan warps our thinking by whispering into our thoughts: "Seek personal empowerment. Believe in yourself. You are your own hero." This appeals to our human nature. We've all seen young children learn basic skills and exclaim, "I did it all by myself!"

Learning life skills and self-sufficiency are necessary and good. The danger lies in thinking we don't need God to get through this life.

You shall have no other gods before Me. (Exodus 20:3)

ARE WE BETTER THAN GOD?

When I was teaching my first graders about the account of creation, they learned that God created the heavens and the earth, the stars, the land, the animals, the plants, and the people. Lastly, we learned that God rested. As I told the story, a sweet girl looked up at me with wide eyes and blurted, "God took a NAP?! Man, I bet He was TIRED!"

Out of the mouths of babes! The almighty God *rested*—not because He was tired, but because He celebrated with Adam and Eve on their first day of life in His glorious, wondrous creation. But here *we* are, running about our day with work, errands, obligations, and activities—day after day without any rest. Are we more powerful than God? Do we have more in the reserves than the One who created us?

A well-known Bible account about idolatry is in Exodus 32: the golden calf. The Israelites were camped out at the bottom of Mount Sinai. Moses had gone up the mountain to receive word from God and bring it back to the people. But he took too long in their eyes—forty days. Do you resonate with the impatience too? Is God not answering your prayer fast enough for you? Me too.

As Moses was away, the people complained to Aaron, who decided to collect everyone's gold, melt it in a fire, and form it into an idol (in the shape of a golden calf). The people set up an altar to worship this calf, not the God of the universe.

There is more to this story, but the point I want to make is this: We can look at this story and say we'd never have done that. We knew Moses was coming back, so we would have kept our eyes on God.

Maybe so, but we have the benefit of knowing the end of this story. I think that more times than not, we behave just like the Israelites. We grow impatient. We don't wait for the Lord to act. We replace Him; it's just not with a golden calf made from fire.

WHAT'S YOUR GOLDEN CALF?

We all have some form of a golden calf in our lives. There's something we turn to, instead of Jesus, when life is hard or when we grow impatient with the way our lives are going. We all have something that we think makes us stronger, better, more invincible.

My golden calf is coffee. My relationship with coffee started innocently. It's delicious and best to drink over a cozy conversation with a friend. When I had my first child, I found myself drinking it more. I would start the day with a cup, have another cup during the morning, and then again maybe in the afternoon. I'd say, "Just need another cup." "I'm so tired, only coffee will fix this." I found myself not being able to go a day without it. Slowly but surely, I started to equate my strength to work or live through a day based on whether I'd have coffee or not.

Now, this habit of coffee isn't bad by itself. As a coffee fanatic, this can be a great thing to enjoy. The concern is when this habit becomes my "savior." This habit that started off innocently had taken a turn to become an idol. I started to look to my coffee to get me through instead of turning to God in prayer or in His Word. I turned to coffee to give me my strength instead of turning to God and using His wisdom to ask

MYTH 8: BE YOUR OWN HERO

others for help or change my lifestyle to allow for more rest. I believed that I was only able to make it through the day or get through a conversation with someone because I'd ingested my coffee for the day.

Another example where we may have a golden calf is the focus on the number of reactions on our social media. Do we equate our worth with how many likes we obtain through a video or photo? Do we spend more time scrolling than we do diving into God's Word? Do we turn down the Bible study group because we are too tired but then spend an hour on our beds scrolling and comparing our profiles to others in our community?

Can you relate? Maybe it's not coffee for you but something else. Maybe it's something you tell yourself you can't go a day without. This could be your phone or social media. This could be a glass of wine at the end of the day. This could be your exercise routine. Our flesh can take something that can be harmless with moderation but use it to an excessiveness that can lead to thoughts that include things such as *Because of this, my life is better.* Instead, we can think, "I'm thankful for this tool, but my strength and identity isn't from this but from God."

Now, to clarify, can you enjoy these things, daily, and know that they're not the source of your strength? Absolutely! This is less about the habit and more about the attitude of our hearts. Do we love these habits more than we love God? If we go back to my coffee habit, I have reduced it to one a day, and I know that the coffee doesn't provide my strength but God does, along with working through caffeine. ;) I want to talk about the times when we replace going to God, through prayer or reading His Word, with an object or activity. Once again, could I be using prayer to get me through the afternoon slump, not another cup of coffee? I want us to look at the motives behind why we do what we do.

FALSE SENSE OF SECURITY

Our world tells us constantly that we can do whatever we want, when we want it, and how. If we disagree, if we say, "Yes, but . . . what about morals, values, right and wrong?" someone will call us out as judgmental and restrictive. As the young guys would say, *"You do you, boo!"*

For the longest time, I never really thought about that saying. I thought, *What's the harm? It's just telling us to be true to ourselves and do what's best for us.* These ideas seem innocent enough on the surface. Maybe the saying *was* innocent and harmless at the beginning. But words like "Hey, make your own decisions—don't let others decide for you" have become "Whatever your heart desires is okay; if it feels good, do it." This mentality has us looking to our fleshly desires and not considering how they align with God's will for us or even how they might affect other people.

It's so easy to start down this slippery slope. A little gossip, a white lie, padding a resume, peeking at porn—as long as no one finds out, what is the harm? We might feel justified in holding a grudge or withholding forgiveness. If we listen to the world and engage in these behaviors, we build an altar for our own ego.

What about behaviors that begin as good things but become the things we place our hope and confidence in? Take exercise and a healthy diet. According to society and research studies, when we eat healthy foods and engage in regular exercise, we can reduce our risks of disease or premature death. As an avid outdoorswoman and major advocate for fresh air and movement, I believe this is a habit that has incredible merit. These habits are good stewardship of the body and mortal life God has given us.

But what happens when we cut out sugar, abstain from alcohol and tobacco, exercise daily, and get plenty of sleep but still get cancer or heart disease or ALS? We might find ourselves saying, "But I did all the right things! Why did this happen to me?" We believe nothing bad will happen to us because we take care of ourselves. You probably know someone who this has happened to. The first thing you might think is *But they were so healthy; it's not fair.*

Just because we take care of our bodies doesn't mean sin and its effects go away. People who do all the "right" things are just as susceptible to the degradation of God's creation as people who have no regard for the sanctity of life. No, by our human understanding and standards, life isn't fair. A nonsmoker gets lung cancer and dies at age 35, while a

MYTH 8: BE YOUR OWN HERO

lifelong smoker lives to age 100. A baby is born with a heart defect that can't be repaired with surgery. A family dies in a car crash.

Putting our faith in the things of this life, in earthly abilities and habits, is like building a house on sand. Believing we can go our own way and be our own (*fill in the blank*) is foolish and even threatens our eternal life. Instead, let us confess our faith in the one true thing: our Rock and Redeemer.

COMFORT FROM HABITS OR FROM GOD?

While we are on the topic of our habits, I want to spend a moment talking about go-to behaviors that bring us comfort. In moderation, things like scrolling social media or having a glass of wine at bedtime are innocent and not a big deal. They even aid our relaxation and provide entertainment.

But when habits replace our devotional practices, worship time, and fellowship with other believers, they become problems. When we look to the comfort of such habits to distract us from our responsibilities and vocations, to self-isolate, or to substitute for interpersonal interaction, we are in a danger zone. When we rely on a meme or trendy video for spiritual food instead of opening our Bible or listening to a sermon, we risk replacing God's truth with culture. Friend, nothing can be a substitute for the Word of God and the work done through the Holy Spirit. No comfort or idol can provide what the triune God can provide for us.

WHAT ARE YOU PUTTING YOUR IDENTITY IN?

In college, I took a class called "Faith and Life." It was required of all students at the college I attended. A discussion in that class forever changed my thinking. It was on the topic "Who are you?" Let's consider that question for a little bit.

"Who are you?"
What came to mind? What was the first word you thought of when you read the question? Was it your profession, your job, or your vocation? Did you say "parent," "teacher," "businessman," or "spouse"? Or did you go with a character trait such as "kind," "caring," or "hardworking"?

When I answered that question the first time, I listed my job and qualities about myself. For nearly the entire class session, we discussed our characteristics and why we believed those things about ourselves. The professor sat and listened to it all, allowing us the freedom to talk through the topic and not saying a word.

Then, finally, he said, "You're all wrong."

I remember thinking, *Wow. Tell us how you really feel about it.* I still chuckle about that. But his next statement is one I'll never forget: "You are a child of God."

We can get so caught up in what our profession is, what our characteristics are, or how society views us that we forget who we truly are and where our identity comes from. We are God's child, first and foremost. Everything else comes from God as blessings to us and how He works through us to glorify His name. Isaiah reminds us in 43:1:

> But now thus says the LORD, He who created you, O Jacob, He who formed you, O Israel: "Fear not, for I have redeemed you; I have called you by name, you are Mine."

God called us by name. We are His and His alone.

> Before I formed you in the womb I knew you. (Jeremiah 1:5)

SUPERHEROES AND HAPPY ENDINGS

Society tells us to believe in ourselves. If we are struggling with how to live our lives, we can see how celebrities live theirs. Videos and television shows and memes would have us believe that if only we follow them, all the happiness in the world is ours!

That's not always a bad thing. What's bad is when we use media and the philosophies and people it celebrates as the guide for our lives. When we turn away from God's Word, we fall prey to defeat. We won't find our hero among the pages and people of the secular world. Society will tell us, however, what it thinks a hero should be. Take a moment to think of your favorite superhero movie. Got it?

What makes the main character of that movie a hero? What qualities

MYTH 8: BE YOUR OWN HERO

does he or she possess? Is she strong? Does he have magical powers? Did he do something amazing or have all the money to buy all the gadgets to protect people?

Superhero movies all have a story arc and a central theme. Something tragic or scary happens. An evil foe is trying to hurt innocent people and take over the world, or a massive disaster happens that only a handful of people can do anything about.

This scenario should be familiar to you. Do you know something where evil comes to seek, kill, and destroy us? Yes. Sunday School for the win again: Satan.

Our battle with Satan isn't won by a Hollywood type of superhero. Our hero is the Son of a carpenter and the Son of the most high God. Our hero was tempted in every way yet lived a sinless life. He slept and ate and wept. He suffered and was beaten. And He died on the cross—for us.

That scene, that superhero action, was the moment of final defeat for the evil foe. Satan lost. Jesus, our true hero, won once for all.

Spend a few minutes on social media or take a peek at a magazine rack in a drug store, and you'll see over and over again the message that we are our own heroes, that we just need to believe in ourselves, and everything will work out. But that's not honoring our God. God, the maker of heaven and earth, sent His Son so that we could have eternal life with Him in heaven. Luke 19:10 reminds us, "For the Son of Man came to seek and to save the lost." Jesus came for you and for me, for our loved ones, and even for our enemies.

Our hero isn't in things like a cup of coffee, a glass of wine, and exercise routine, or whatever else our flesh tries to tell us is important. No, our hero is Jesus. He is the ultimate hero with the ultimate victory over death and the devil.

WHO IS THE IDOL IN YOUR FAITH WALK?

We know not to look to Hollywood for our wisdom. We know deep down not to listen to society, but we still fall down the rabbit hole every once in a while by rejecting the secular world and lifting up a famous

Christian or even our church. For instance, have you relied on the latest social media post of a Christian speaker or blogger instead of reading God's Word for yourself? It's certainly true that God is working through many of these people. He has gifted them with a voice and a platform that furthers His Gospel message. Our world needs more people speaking out about Jesus and His sacrifice on the cross. These voices can be a help and a guide, but they should not be *the* guide or *the* help over Scripture.

We can see the same issue happening in the Bible too. In 1 Corinthians 1, Paul wrote to the church in Corinth. Corinth then was a lot like our world today. One of the issues Paul addressed in his letter was division and disagreement in the church. Paul reminded them to be of the same mind and the same judgment (see 1 Corinthians 1:10).

Each one of you says, "I follow Paul," or "I follow Apollos," or "I follow Cephas," or "I follow Christ." Is Christ divided? Was Paul crucified for you? Or were you baptized in the name of Paul?" (vv. 12–13)

Let's focus on this part: "Was Paul crucified for you? Or were you baptized in the name of Paul?" The Corinthians were holding allegiance to someone who shared the faith instead of looking to the One who was the reason for the faith in the first place. Paul isn't with us today, but we could replace his name with the latest Instagram profile we turn to for wisdom and insight when we are feeling defeated or worn down.

When we turn to influencers first or instead of opening God's Word, we risk making them an idol.

"You shall have no other gods before Me." (Exodus 20:3)

You may be like me and read that and go, "Of course not!" I'm not worshiping a crystal or a sun god or some feeling in the wind. Yet could we be sharing a social media post or meme that sounds solid but doesn't track with the Word of God? I pray that I'm always held accountable. I pray that I have colleagues, friends, family members, and church workers who hold me accountable to God's Word as I endeavor to be a helpful light on the internet.

We could take this a step further and consider how we think about our

MYTH 8: BE YOUR OWN HERO

pastors. Paul wrote, "For when one says, 'I follow Paul,' and another, 'I follow Apollos,' are you not being merely human?" (1 Corinthians 3:4). In the early church, when the world was volatile, some aligned themselves with certain Christian leaders instead of with Jesus specifically. Paul reminded them that when they say they follow him or Apollos, they are saying they are following a sinner and not the sinless Son of God. Friend, we don't have to put our faith in a flawed human, even one who is an authority on Scripture and in the church. Instead, we put our faith and the hope of eternal life in the man who lived a perfect life and died for our sins, defeating death and the devil, and rising again: Jesus. The Bible—with all its authority and truth—is readily accessible to us.

But it's easy to fall into the same trap the people in Corinth were in. Our pastors have a divine call to preach, teach, and lead us. God has literally given them this work and has equipped and trained them to follow Him and guide us to do the same. But we have a responsibility here too.

When Preston and I moved to Omaha, for the first time in our lives, there was more than one Lutheran church to go to. While we decided which church to attend, my husband kept asking, "Do they preach the Law and Gospel? Do they stay true to God's Word?" Yes, there were many congregations that did just this, so we chose one that's closer to where we live and that offers a service that aligns with our worship style.

The point of my story is this: There are many churches that are cool and new, have great music and coffee bars, and still proclaim God's Word and faithfully administer the Sacraments. But there is a growing number of churches built around a pastor and not on the foundation of Christ Jesus. May we discern the difference with the help of the wisdom of God.

ONLY ONE TRUE GOD

We have a hero, not a fictional character or a charismatic influencer. Our God loved us so much that He sent His Son to die for us so we may be reconciled to Him now and forever. The prophet Isaiah speaks on the foolishness of idols:

> Thus says the LORD, the King of Israel and His Redeemer, the LORD of hosts: "I am the first and the I am the last; besides Me there is no

god. Who is like Me? Let him proclaim it. Let him declare and set it before Me, since I appointed an ancient people. Let them declare what is to come and what will happen. Fear not, nor be afraid; have I not told you from of old and declared it? And you are My witnesses! Is there a God besides Me? There is no Rock; I know not any." All who fashion idols are nothing, and the things they delight in do not profit. Their witnesses neither see nor know that they may be put to shame. Who fashions a god or casts an idol that is profitable for nothing? (Isaiah 44:6–10)

The Lord God is first and last. We can hold up any idol against Him, and He will always overcome. God will always be the one true God. We can try to replace Him with sayings, habits, or other people, but when trials and suffering come (and they will), only He will stand true and be our strength. Only He is our hope.

Because it will be revealed by fire, and the fire will test what sort of work each one has done. (1 Corinthians 3:13)

WHAT IS OUR FOUNDATION?

David reminded us why we worship and rely on God:

The LORD is my rock and my fortress and my deliverer, my God, my rock, in whom I take refuge, my shield, and the horn of my salvation, my stronghold. (Psalm 18:2)

As I read this verse, I found myself thinking about the "horn of my salvation." This is not a popular phrase today. When we think of God and His strength, we often hear rock, fortress, and refuge. But the horn of our salvation is not as common. This led me to dive deeper. According to Oxford Reference, the horn of salvation[19] speaks to the saving power of the king, royal saving power, now belonging to the Messiah. Our King is Jesus. Jesus saves us, and through Him and His sacrifice on the cross, we have victory over death—He is our salvation.

For no one can lay a foundation other than that which is laid, which is Jesus Christ. (1 Corinthians 3:11)

We can try to replace our foundation with our own flesh, with things

MYTH 8: BE YOUR OWN HERO

from the secular world or from other people around us, but these things are not the true foundation, and none of them can support us.

> Everyone then who hears these words of Mine and does them will be like a wise man who built his house on the rock. And the rain fell, and the floods came, and the winds blew and beat on that house, but it did not fall, because it had been found on the rock. And everyone who hears these words of Mine and does not do them will be like a foolish man who built his house on the sand. And the rain fell, and the floods came, and the winds blew and beat against that house, and it fell, and great was the fall of it. (Matthew 7:24-27)

This lesson from Jesus is a favorite of kids, but it's especially important to adults. I pray that we aren't too proud to look foolish to this world and instead admit our weakness and inadequacy when we try to find our strength from within.

> Jesus said to them, "Have you never read in the Scriptures: 'The stone that the builders rejected has become the cornerstone; this was the Lord's doing, and it is marvelous in our eyes'?" (Matthew 21:42)

Our foundation is one that the world does not understand, but we do not put our hope in this world. No, dear friend, we put it in Jesus, who sacrificed Himself on the cross for us.

GOD SENT JESUS FOR US

> For God so loved the world, that He gave His only Son, that whoever believes in Him should not perish but have eternal life. (John 3:16)

There is one true God. Even the devil knows this. God the Father sent His Son to die for us. Only Jesus lived a perfect life, free from sin, was crucified, died, and was buried. Only Jesus defeated death and the devil and rose again on the third day to bring us eternal life with Him. Only Jesus is seated at the right hand of God.

> For the Son of Man came to seek and to save the lost. (Luke 19:10)

We were lost in our sin, separated from God and condemned by our sin. That sounds harsh, doesn't it? And if the devil had his way, we would stay there. But we were given faith in Jesus through the work of the Holy Spirit, and that faith is refreshed and sustained by the Holy Spirit. God will never forsake us, even if we do at times feel forgotten, even if we echo the prayer of David in Psalm 42:9: "Why have You forgotten me?" Friend, God hasn't forgotten you and never will. He continuously calls to you in His Word and loves you unconditionally in the work of His Son. And He sends us the Comforter—the Holy Spirit—who sustains our faith and reminds us of our peace and hope.

PRAYER:

Heavenly Father,
Thank You for loving me and forming me. Thank You for sending Your Son, Jesus, to die on the cross for our sins so that we can live with You in heaven. Forgive me for placing my trust in things such as my habits or a social media influencer. Forgive me for going to social media before going to the truth that's in Your Word. Forgive me for breaking the First Commandment. Help me, Father, seek Your wisdom and strength and find truth and peace in Your Word for me, the Bible. Help me use discernment when listening to voices outside of Your Word. Make Your will known to me through the preaching and reading of Your Word.
In Jesus' name. Amen.

GENTLE REMINDERS:

- Our faith is not in something or a sinner. It is in Jesus.

- Take inventory of your habits. Do they get in the way of your relationship with God?

- Incorporate spiritual habits that put your focus on your Savior: prayer, reading God's Word, worshiping with fellow believers, and receiving the Lord's Supper.

- You are a child of God. God calls you by name.

MYTH 8: BE YOUR OWN HERO

JOURNAL PROMPT:

What or who have you made an idol? Why do you believe you've made that thing or person into an idol?

Conclusion

> In the beginning was the Word, and the Word was with God, and the Word was God. He was in the beginning with God. All things were made through Him, and without Him was not any thing made that was made. In Him was life, and the life was the light of men. The light shines in the darkness, and the darkness has not overcome it. (John 1:1–5)

Our church's Christmas Eve service was this past weekend. This is a time when we read straight from Scripture and sing hymns about this special time in the Church Year. That night, our family fast-walked into church, sat down with an exasperated sigh, and took up an entire pew and a half. Throughout the service, we passed grandchildren back and forth and dispensed snacks without limit. Getting our household to church is always a roller coaster, but in the midst of that chaos was Jesus. He was present in that Divine Service, reminding us of His story and His gift of peace for us. We can rest in that story, where we have a hope that is everlasting and is so much stronger than any saying or trend.

As our pastor read the Scripture passages, John 1 stood out to me. These beautiful words give us the wisdom that so many people are looking for. We are looking for peace and hope as we navigate this broken world. Our culture fills us with phrases, sayings, and comments that draw our eyes to the latest trend, a "new" thought that captivates us and wants us to believe that happiness and peace are as easy as saying a few generic words.

John reminds us that we don't need to go searching at the local craft store or social media site to find hope. From the beginning of time, our triune God has been present in all places. Through Him, all things are created. Without Jesus, we have nothing. With Him, there is light.

When darkness threatens to overtake us, when we are bogged down in sin and shame, Jesus is the light that keeps shining. His light is continuous; it will never grow dim and never go out.

CONCLUSION

God is faithful, by whom you were called into the fellowship of His Son, Jesus Christ our Lord. (1 Corinthians 1:9)

But the Lord is faithful. He will establish you and guard you against the evil one. (2 Thessalonians 3:3)

Jesus seeks us relentlessly. He draws us to Himself and gives us comfort, hope, and the promise of eternal life with Him. He defends us against the darkness and deceit of Satan. As John reminds us, Jesus is with us through pain, suffering, and despair. He is with us in joy and laughter and celebration.

Friend, He was with us in the beginning. He is with us now. And He will be with us forever.

Amen!

NOTES

NOTES

ENDNOTES

1. "What Is Grounding," University of New Hampshire, https://www.unh.edu/pacs/what-grounding (accessed February 7, 2024).

2. Sunghyon Kyeong, Joohan Kim, Dae Jin Kim, Hesun Erin Kim, and Jae-Jin Kim, "Effects of Gratitude Meditation on Neural Network Functional Connectivity and Brain-Heart Coupling," *Scientific Reports* 7, July 11, 2017, https://doi.org/10.1038/s41598-017-05520-9 (accessed February 7, 2024).

3. Saul Levine, "Psychological and Social Aspects of Resilience: A Synthesis of Risks and Resources," *Dialogues in Clinical Neuroscience* 5, no. 3, September 2005, https://www.ncbi.nlm.nih.gov/pmc/articles/PMC3181637/ (accessed February 7, 2024).

4. Angela Lee Duckworth, "Grit: The Power of Passion and Perseverance," April 2013, TED Talk Education, https://www.ted.com/talks/angela_lee_duckworth_grit_the_power_of_passion_and_perseverance (accessed February 7, 2024).

5. "Dissociative Amnesia," Cleveland Clinic, September 18, 2023, https://my.clevelandclinic.org/health/diseases/9789-dissociative-amnesia (accessed February 9, 2024).

6. Claire Gecewicz, "'New Age' Beliefs Common among Both Religious and Nonreligious Americans," Pew Research Center, October 1, 2018, https://www.pewresearch.org/short-reads/2018/10/01/new-age-beliefs-common-among-both-religious-and-nonreligious-americans/ (accessed February 9, 2024).

7. Gecewicz, "'New Age' Beliefs Common among Both Religious and Nonreligious Americans."

8. Dan Witters, "U.S. Depression Rates Reach New Highs," *Gallup News*, May 17, 2023, https://news.gallup.com/poll/505745/depression-rates-reach-new-highs.aspx (accessed February 9, 2024).

9. Witters, "U.S. Depression Rates Reach New Highs."

10. Suniya S. Luthar and Bronwyn E. Becker, "Privileged but Pressured? A Study of Affluent Youth," *Society for Research in Child Development* 73, no. 5, January 28, 2003, http://srcd.onlinelibrary.wiley.com/doi/abs/10.1111/1467-8624.00492 (accessed February 12, 2024).

11 Matthew A. Killingsworth, Daniel Kahneman, and Barbara Mellers, "Income and Emotional Well-Being: A Conflict Resolved," *Proceedings of the National Academy of Sciences of the United States of America* 120, no. 10, March 1, 2023, https://www.pnas.org/doi/10.1073/pnas.2208661120 (accessed February 9, 2024).

12 Dai Sugimoto, Sarah S. Jackson, David R. Howell, William P. Meehan III, and Andrea Stracciolini, "Association between Training Volume and Lower Extremity Overuse Injuries in Young Female Athletes: Implications for Early Sports Specialization," *The Physician and Sportsmedicine* 47, no. 2, 2019, https://www.tandfonline.com/doi/abs/10.1080/00913847.2018.1546107 (accessed February 9, 2024).

13 "Emotional Exhaustion during Times of Unrest," Mayo Clinic Health System, July 30, 2020, https://www.mayoclinichealthsystem.org/hometown-health/speaking-of-health/emotional-exhaustion-during-times-of-unrest (accessed February 9, 2024).

14 "Highlights of the Finnish Educational System," Finland Center Foundation, February 20, 2020, https://www.finlandcenter.org/fcf-blog/2020/2/20/highlights-of-the-finnish-educational-system (accessed February 9, 2024).

15 Deborah Farmer Kris, "How Movement and Gestures Can Improve Student Learning," *MindShift*, June 29, 2021, https://www.kqed.org/mindshift/58051/how-movement-and-gestures-can-improve-student-learning (accessed February 9, 2024).

16 "Boston Celtics Head Coach Relies on Faith after Losing in Conference Finals," Movieguide, May 31, 2023, https://www.movieguide.org/news-articles/boston-celtics-head-coach-relies-on-faith-after-losing-in-conference-finals.html (accessed February 9, 2024).

17 Daniel Heimpel, "Abused Children May Become Abusive Adults," *The Imprint*, March 14, 2014, https://imprintnews.org/research-news/abused-children-may-become-abusive-adults/5548 (accessed April 4, 2024).

18 Steven L. Berman, "Identity and Trauma," *Journal of Traumatic Stress Disorders and Treatments* 5, no. 2, April 2016, https://www.scitechnol.com/peer-review/identity-and-trauma-FBG5.php?article_id=5034 (accessed February 9, 2024).

19 "Horn of Salvation," Oxford University Press, https://www.oxfordreference.com/display/10.1093/oi/authority.20110803095945344 (accessed February 9, 2024).